THE GLOBAL
NEGOTIATOR

THE GLOBAL NEGOTIATOR

*Building Strong Business Relationships
Anywhere in the World*

Trenholme J. Griffin
and
W. Russell Daggatt

HarperBusiness
A Division of HarperCollins*Publishers*

International Standard Book Number: 0–88730–434–6

Library of Congress Catalog Card Number 90-4587

Printed in the United States of America

Library of Congress Cataloging-in-Publication Data
Griffin, Trenholme J.
 The global negotiator / by Trenholme J. Griffin and W. Russell Daggatt.
  p.   cm.
 Includes bibliographical references and index.
 ISBN 0-88730-434-6
 1. Negotiation in business. I. Daggatt, W. Russell. II. Title.
HD58.6.G75   1990   90-4587
658.4—dc20   CIP

92 93 NK/HC 9 8 7 6 5 4 3 2

Contents

Acknowledgments

This book would not have been possible without the generous assistance of many people. We are also indebted to people who have acted as mentors to us. Among those who have contributed to our careers or to this book are Young Moo Kim, Jeff Jones, and Ken Jennings in Seoul; Richard Rabinowitz and Michael "Buck" Tharp in Tokyo; Richard Marshall and Steve Miller in Sydney; John Waugh in Auckland; Gene Flynn in Jakarta; Joe Supsinskas in Hong Kong; Vera Sparre in Munich; Griffith Way and Rick Dodd in Seattle; and Gerald Grinstein in Fort Worth. Special thanks are appropriate for Nancy Griffin for her support, editorial assistance, and patience.

The authors are active collectors of anecdotes and stories, particularly those which are amusing, insightful, or unusual. Interested readers may send their stories to the authors at 5400 COLUMBIA CENTER, 701 FIFTH AVENUE, SEATTLE, WA 98104-7078, FACSIMILE: (206)623-7022.

THE GLOBAL NEGOTIATOR

1

Introduction

It appears to your majesty's slave that we are very deficient in means, and have not the shells and rocket used by the barbarians. We must, therefore, adopt other methods to stop them, which will be easy, as they have opened negotiations.

—Kee-Shen: *Ministerial report to the Emperor of China during the Opium War with Great Britain, March 1841*

What This Book Is About

John Kenneth Galbraith has said, "Sex apart, negotiation is the most common and problematic involvement of one person with another, and the two activities are not unrelated." Few aspects of human interaction do not involve negotiation. We negotiate nearly constantly with our family, friends, co-workers, customers, and clients. Studies have shown that a typical senior manager in an American business spends at least 20 percent of his or her working day negotiating. The percentage of time spent negotiating by executives involved in international business is even higher. Because we begin to negotiate soon after birth, we do so largely without conscious awareness of the process. Adding to our lack of awareness regarding the negotiation process is an elaborate and unwritten etiquette that has developed over time. Because most of us understand this etiquette, much of our behavior in a negotiation is intuitive. As long as we are operating in our familiar cultural context, an

1

intuitive negotiating style can function with a workable degree of success.

But what happens to this process in an international context? Fundamental differences emerge. There are substantive differences, concerning interests, needs, values, ethics, and goals. There are also stylistic differences, which include etiquette, customs, rituals, and other behavioral habits. An effective international negotiator deals with substantive differences by becoming **conscious** of the negotiation process and with stylistic differences by abandoning an intuitive methodology. The best way to deal with differences, substantive or stylistic, is to become **aware** of the negotiation process. A major theme of this book is that increasing your awareness of the process, by itself, will make you a better negotiator.

The other major theme of this book is that successful international negotiation requires a "relationship orientation" rather than a "deal orientation." Americans tend heavily toward a deal orientation, while most other cultures are comparatively more relationship oriented. To a significant extent, this reflects the mobile and individualistic nature of U.S. society. The traditional social structures of family, community, and religion have increasingly been replaced with a web of situational relationships between individuals represented and enforced through legal mechanisms. This places the emphasis on a "deal," representing a single situational relationship between individuals or companies that may or may not extend beyond the immediate matter at hand. This deal is set forth in a legal contract and the parties are expected to abide by that contract.

There are two problems with the deal orientation. The first is the practical difficulty of crafting, interpreting, and enforcing a legal agreement across multiple legal and governmental jurisdictions. The other more significant problem is the dynamic nature of the world. A deal orientation is essentially static in nature, while a relationship orientation is dynamic in nature. For both these reasons, working on developing a solid, mutually beneficial relationship is a better approach to a dynamic global environment than trying to craft a series of "airtight" agreements reflecting interests at a single static point in time.

What This Book Is Not About

This book doesn't pretend to offer a general theory of negotiation. There is no one archetypal negotiation. The dynamic of each negotiation is unique, and differences between individual negotiations can overwhelm similarities. Negotiating with your spouse may or may not bear resemblance to a superpower arms negotiation. Negotiation is a skill best learned from experience. Yet most of us would seek to avoid the hard lessons of experience by learning from those who have traveled this road before us. While this book doesn't provide a road map for every negotiation, it does seek to distill some insight and judgment from a vast collective experience. Our own experience includes negotiating a wide range of business transactions, including joint ventures, distributorships, and technology licenses for companies such as IBM, American Express, Hyundai, Toshiba, Northwest Airlines, Texas Instruments, Procter & Gamble, Nike, Flying Tigers, and Daewoo.

One of our motivations for writing this book was the tendency of other books on the subject to presume to identify negotiating styles of whatever country is the subject of the work. Propounding a list of generalizations about a culture encourages the reader to go into a negotiation struggling to recall these profound prejudices rather than focusing on the statements and interests of the other party. It may be true that the Japanese tend to use intermediaries more, that Mexicans tend to focus on maintaining honor, that the French frequently value principle over result, that time tends to be less important in Africa, that Germans tend to place more importance on nomenclature and titles, and that various cultures are rife with corruption. But no list can create consciousness or awareness. What is needed is a skill and not an exhaustive compilation of generalizations. Indeed, generalizations like those listed above reinforce and exacerbate a negotiator's tendency to make false assumptions.

Rather than create a country-by-country laundry list of cultural generalizations, the authors have created an inventory of areas where cultures **tend** to differ. We have found that the following areas require a negotiator to be particularly careful and observant:

1. The nature of the process (for example, give and take or take it or leave it).
2. The value of time.
3. The importance of etiquette, protocol, and ceremony.
4. The decision-making process.
5. The importance of principle and honor.
6. The use of intermediaries.
7. The make-up of the negotiating team.
8. The appropriate level of trust.
9. The importance of individual versus group aspirations.
10. The appropriate level of risk.
11. The appropriate manner of communicating information or proposals.
12. The appropriate form of final agreement.

This book is also not a cultural encyclopedia that tells you what to wear to high tea in London, how to pour beer in Korea, what to bring a hostess as a gift in São Paulo, or how to cross your legs in Saudi Arabia (don't show the soles of your shoes). Writing such an encyclopedia would require more volumes than the Oxford English Dictionary. No person can learn or remember every potential cultural faux pas. Rather than assembling a huge cargo of cultural trivia, focus on awareness and assemble cultural knowledge as the need arises on a situational basis.

Why This Book Is Important

In adapting to an international business environment, an American may be at a disadvantage to his or her foreign counterpart. Many foreign business executives have been doing business internationally since they began doing business. The proximity of foreign markets and the opportunities they offered could not easily be ignored. If the opportunities did not provide a sufficient "carrot," neighboring competition provided the "stick." Through experience and practice, they typically will have become more conscious of the negotiating process. They should also have learned to abandon an intuitive style of negotiation in order to account for cultural variations. Because of America's blissful geographic isolation, the international negotiation skills of Americans in general lag behind those of foreigners. The United States emerged from World War II with few economic scars and a booming economy. Taking advantage of our abundant natural resources, leadership in industrial technology, and undamaged industrial facilities, the United States was able to ignore foreign competition. For close to three decades America had the world's strongest economy and largest domestic market, encouraging a more general cultural isolation.

America's businesses must learn to function in a global economy characterized by intense economic competition transcending borders if they are to be successful. The business leaders of the next millennium will operate on a worldwide scale. The increasing technical sophistication of foreign competitors and the difficulty of recovering rising research and development costs solely in the United States have forced a whole new group of American business executives to look to foreign countries as a source of revenue. Even those American companies that may have been successful importers or exporters in the past will have to sharpen their negotiating skills as a result of increasing foreign competition.

The move to capture revenues in foreign markets is affecting all types of U.S. companies. A few statistics illustrate the importance of international business to U.S. companies:

- Procter & Gamble, a classic consumer products company, generated 36 percent of its total revenues from overseas sales in 1988. In 1984 Procter & Gamble was active in 27 countries. In 1989 they were active in 48. Executives at Procter & Gamble expect foreign sales to account for over half of revenues in the 1990s.

- H. J. Heinz earns more than 40 percent of its profits overseas.

- Coca-Cola Co. made more money on soft drinks in both Japan and Europe than it did in the United States in 1988.
- Over half of General Motors's income in 1989 came from non–United States sources. General Motors owns over 40 percent of Isuzu and half of Korea's Daewoo Motors. Ford owns 25 percent of Mazda and makes trucks with Volkswagen in Brazil. Chrysler owns 24 percent of Mitsubishi Motors.
- IBM obtained approximately 60 percent of its revenues from overseas in 1989.
- Campbell Soup Co. generated 27 percent of sales from overseas and has aggressive plans to increase this amount to 40 percent in the early 1990s.
- Overall, exports from the U.S. as a whole rose by more than 12.4 percent in 1989 to $364 billion, making the U.S. the world's largest exporter. The U.S. is also the world's largest importer due to its $459.5 billion of imports in 1989. U.S. companies spent $48.9 billion in 1989 in purchasing foreign assets. At the end of 1989, the total value of U.S. overseas holdings was $368.1 billion.

When faced with the difficulties and costs associated with doing business overseas, many American businesses have concluded that it is too difficult, too risky, and not worth the trouble. Whether American business executives like it or not, commercial isolation is no longer possible. Even if you don't go to them, they are coming to you. Foreign businesses are invading U.S. markets in unprecedented numbers. They are entering our markets, both by selling their products and by purchasing existing businesses in the United States. Names like Sony, Perrier, and Mercedes are as familiar as General Electric, Pepsi, and Ford. Even supposedly made-in-the-U.S.A. products like the IBM Personal Computer and the Remington Shaver contain foreign components. The following statistics illustrate the increasing presence of foreign companies in the United States:

- Foreign investment in the United States during 1989 exceeded $65 billion. Foreign assets in the United States increased to $390 billion in 1989. Japanese direct investment in the United States increased by 12.8 billion in 1989, bringing total Japanese direct investment in the United States to $66.1 billion. That surpasses Canadian assets in the United States of $29.7 billion and Dutch assets of $122.8 billion but still lags far behind British assets of $122.8 billion.

- Foreigners now own U.S. companies that sell products or services under brand names like Firestone, Jergens, Shell, Lipton, Singer, Shaklee, CBS Records, RCA Records, Doubleday, Purina, Conair, Talbots, Pillsbury, Baskin-Robbins, Columbia Pictures, Wilson, Smith Corona, Brooks Brothers, Thermos, Alka-Seltzer, Good Humor, Westin Hotels, Carnation, and even Harper & Row.

- Over a quarter million Americans were working for Japanese employers as of the end of 1988, and this figure is expected to exceed one million in the 1990s.

- The share of the American banking market held by the more than 200 foreign banks operating in the United States rose to 21 percent in 1989 from 10 percent in 1982.

- In 1974 the United States was developing 70 percent of the world's advanced technology. By 1994 the share of the United States in this vital area is expected to be less than 30 percent. America's share of global car manufacturing has fallen from 75 percent in 1960 to 25 percent in 1988.

- A 1988 analysis by Coldwell Banker estimated that 46 percent of all office space in Los Angeles is owned by foreigners, as is 39 percent in Houston and 21 percent in New York.

- One out of every six production jobs depends on foreign trade. Four out of five new jobs in the United States are created as a result of foreign trade.

As the globalization of the economy of the United States and other countries intensifies, it will become increasingly important that business executives improve their international negotiation skills. The need for individuals who can successfully negotiate in a multicultural setting will exist at all organizational levels in the 1990s and beyond. In the corporate setting, lower-level managers will increasingly need international negotiation skills.

The Structure of the Book

This book's discussion of global negotiating skills consists of two sections. The first section is intended to develop your negotiating skills. This discussion explores the nature of a relationship as the link allowing both parties to create and claim value. The second section will identify some winning strategies and tactics that can be used in international negotiation. A four-stage model is set out to increase your understanding of the negotiation process: (1) preparation; (2) bargaining; (3) ceremony; and (4) implementation and dynamic renegotiations. As each of these four stages in the negotiating process is discussed, specific problems and behaviors encountered in the international context will be portrayed through the experiences of those who have sailed before you in these often disquieting seas.

Negotiation is not a science that allows variables to be quantified and a precise result calculated according to a formula. There is no "right" way to negotiate. Because each individual is unique, no single negotiating style will yield the best result. Every person has strengths and weaknesses that will affect his or her negotiating ability. Your own analytical ability, economic resources, industriousness, communication skills, and experience will also come into play in determining the outcome. Whatever your personal style or resources, the more you understand the negotiation process, how this process plays itself out in an international context, and the common forms of gamesmanship that you may encounter, the greater your chance of obtaining a favorable result.

This book is written for both novice and experienced international negotiators. Among the latter group, the wise know that the learning process never stops. They are constantly seeking to learn from those who are more experienced or skillful. Especially in the international context, it is important to look for new approaches as well as new perspectives on familiar problems. And becoming more conscious of the negotiation process will help ensure that intuitive patterns are not repeated in inappropriate settings.

There is no better teacher than experience (although we obviously hope this book will come in a close second). The more opportunities you have to negotiate, the better your negotiation skills will become. To quote the Soviet founder Nikolai Lenin, "One must spend time in the water in order to swim." Try seeking out opportunities in your business and personal life to hone the skills encouraged here. We hope this book will be helpful even for those whose negotiating experiences may never extend beyond their immediate families. Good negotiation skills will help you achieve your goals, whatever those goals may be.

2

Building Global Bridges

A bridge is bad if it is shorter than the width of the stream.

—German Proverb

I would rather have goodwill and cooperation than logic.

—Jawaharlal Nehru

BUILD RELATIONSHIPS; DON'T DO DEALS

When pressed to distill our international negotiating experience down to a single glib maxim, our response is immediate: When doing business internationally, think of the process as building a relationship, not doing a deal. Of course, not all negotiations entail building a relationship. When you are negotiating with a terrorist, your primary objective may be to avoid any future relationship. Nonetheless, our experience has taught us that overestimating the value of building long-term relationships is much less of a danger than overestimating the primacy of short-term considerations.

One of the major premises of this book is that people are essentially the same, but cultures are not. International negotiation is unique because cultural differences create barriers to agreement and opportunities for conflict that would not exist in a negotiation between compatriots. A bridge must be built to span these differences. This bridge is the **relationship** be-

11

tween the parties. Generally, the better the relationship, the more likely the negotiation will result in a successful outcome. Because these global bridges must deal with greater cultural differences, they are usually harder and more expensive to build. Once constructed, however, they can be used to transport great gains.

Understanding cultural differences is vital to the success of an international negotiation. Deep cultural chasms may be hidden by the outward manifestations of culture that have become increasingly uniform throughout the industrialized world. People may wear business suits, listen to Michael Jackson, and watch François Truffaut films, while their traditional values, beliefs, and opinions remain more or less intact. While easily observable racial differences may tend to make one sensitive to cultural differences, beware of making opposite assumptions. Americans of European heritage may be dangerously prone to assume that only language and half a dozen time zones distinguish them from their European counterparts. Cross-cultural understanding requires that you question all cultural assumptions, overcome your own ethnocentrism, and above all else, don't judge.

Any relationship is dynamic and constantly changing; it is a process, not a status. It also should not be confused with similarity of goals, interests or opinions. Negotiators can disagree strongly and yet have a good relationship. The quality in a relationship depends on the ability of negotiators to identify and reconcile shared and conflicting interests as well as establish mechanisms for creating and sharing value. The ability of the negotiators to establish and respect limits can also increase the quality of a relationship.

Negotiators who have an effective ongoing relationship will be able to **agree to disagree** and not have the disagreement negatively affect their relationship. Understanding another person's beliefs does not require acceptance of those beliefs. Conversely, intolerance of personal differences does not make a person stronger or superior to the other.

The late Leon Festinger, a scholar of communications, coined the term *cognitive dissonance* to describe the conflict we feel when a relationship is challenged by differences of opinion. The theory of cognitive dissonance holds that people strive for agreement between their affinity for another person and the beliefs and opinions of that person. If dissonance develops in that relationship, a person will either change his own position with regard to the offending belief or opinion, discount the importance of the matter, or lessen his affinity for the other person. If, for example, your spouse is campaigning ardently for some candidate you detest, you are likely to mellow a bit on the offending politico, dismiss somewhat the importance of the electoral process, cool toward the mate, or some combination of the above. The degree to which this process occurs depends on the strength of the relationship and the extent of the conflict.

The theory of cognitive dissonance is really just an arcane academic elaboration of a bit of everyday folk wisdom. Peter Barfield, the Chairman of International Computers, Ltd., distributes a card to all employees who deal with Fujitsu, his company's partner in Japan. One of the admonitions on the card explains how cognitive dissonance affects relationships. It states in plain terms: "Get to know your opposite numbers at all levels socially. Friends take longer to fall out."

The importance of spending time together to develop a relationship with your negotiating counterpart was driven home to one of the authors in a protracted negotiation with a Japanese group. The Japanese were part of an ambitious project to develop the world's largest retail space devoted exclusively to outdoor recreational activity and related products. The retail complex, to be named The Great Outdoors, would occupy over 145,000 square feet in the basement of the Osaka railway station, through which over a million people pass every day. The author represented one of several U.S. companies the Japanese had sought out to lend their names, products, or expertise to the project (the United States is very much associated in Japan with the great outdoors).

The Japanese had arranged their contacts with the U.S. companies through a U.S. consultant, the former CEO of a major U.S. outdoor equipment company, who dutifully scheduled a full agenda of meetings with the U.S. companies for the Japanese on each of their many trips to the United States. Despite several such meetings spread over six months, the author felt that little progress was being made in his negotiations with the Japanese. It so happened that these negotiations were taking place at the same time that this book was being written. In a case of "doctor heal thyself," the author reviewed the collected jumble of the nascent manuscript and came upon his own injunction: Build relationships; don't do deals. That was it. Several meetings had taken place, all carefully orchestrated by the consultant, but no time had been spent with the Japanese outside those meetings. No relationship was developing.

The author called the consultant and asked if the Japanese were free for dinner that night. As was the case most nights, the consultant had planned to have dinner alone with his Japanese clients, but he readily agreed to include the author in the evening revelries. The dinner at an elegant Berkeley restaurant stretched out nearly four hours, during which time the author and the Japanese developed an affinity based on shared interests unrelated to the deal they had discussed that day. Unfortunately, the end of the evening was marred by an ugly incident involving persistent racist abuse of the Japanese on the part of a couple of very drunk Neanderthals at the adjoining table. As if to confirm the impression of America created by Hollywood westerns, the confrontation culminated in the consultant taking a swing at one of the Neanderthals who had directed a racist and sexually offensive comment at a young woman who was assisting the consultant with this project. After the potential combatants had been separated and dispersed, the Japanese appeared a bit shaken, but were thrilled by this firsthand experience of the Wild West. The incident, by drawing the Japanese and their American companions together against a sinister external threat, seemed to solidify the relationship that had developed so auspiciously earlier in the evening. It is no coincidence that the negotiations with the company the author was representing progressed rapidly thereafter. Meanwhile, negotiations between the Japanese and the other U.S. companies continued to drag on at their lethargic pace.

Just as it is important to strengthen relationships with friends, so it is also necessary to nurture relations with adversaries. After British General Burgoyne surrendered his sword to General Gates after the victory of the American Revolutionary Army at Saratoga, the British officers were given a fine meal and plenty of wine. This action was no doubt a surprise to individuals of the "punish your enemies" school of thought. General Gates was a diplomat as well as a military officer and knew that war is the failure of diplomacy. Good communication and goodwill are attractive alternatives to force in furthering one's end. The proverb "keep your friends close, but your enemies closer" aptly summarizes this principle.

It is important to distinguish between negotiating points that impact the relationship and negotiating points that concern substantive issues. When the negotiation relates to issues like trust, emotions, and perception, relationship issues are involved. When the negotiation concerns issues like quality, prices, or technology transfer, substantive issues are involved. The importance of this difference will become evident as you become more aware of the process of an international negotiation.

FOCUS ON INTERESTS, NOT POSITIONS

Let us not be blind to our differences—but let us also direct attention to our common interests and the means by which those differences can be resolved.

—John F. Kennedy

Interests shouldn't be confused with positions. Interests are one's needs and aspirations that provide the underlying motivation for the negotiation. Positions are adopted by negotiators to advance their interests. There may be any number of positions by which one's interests may be advanced. Focusing on the position rather than the interest is confusing the means with the end.

In one negotiation in the early 1980s, a Taiwanese manufacturer was locked in a dispute with an American importer over how many models of its bicycles it would produce. The American importer wanted four different models, to give its customers greater selection. The Taiwanese company wanted to produce only two models, to keep tooling, inventory, and other manufacturing costs down. The position of the Taiwanese company was that it would produce only two models, while the underlying interest was to keep manufacturing costs down. The position of the American importer was that it wanted four models, while its underlying interest was to increase its profits by selling more bicycles. As long as the negotiators focused on these positions, the dispute could be resolved only through concessions by one or both sides. But an interest-oriented examination of the dispute leads to the question: How can the higher cost of manufacturing four models be allocated between the American importer and the Taiwanese manufacturer? In this example, the parties were able to devise a formula that increased the unit cost of the different models to reflect the Taiwanese manufacturer's increased manufacturing cost. The interests of the Taiwanese were achieved by the solution—profit per unit remained constant. The interests of the American importer were also met—it sold more units at higher prices which more than offset the increased manufacturing costs.

Another example of a negotiation in which a solution was found by focusing on interests rather than positions occurred in Moscow. An American company was negotiating with the Soviet State Committee on Science and Technology concerning the importation of computers. The Soviets had introduced a standard form contract that contained terms that were totally unacceptable to the Americans. The Soviets were intransigent in their insistence that this contract be used. Looking at the positions of the parties, there appeared to be an irreconcilable problem. Fortunately, the American negotiators were able to ascertain the underlying interest of the Soviets. If the language of the form contract was altered in any way, it would be necessary to process it through numerous levels in the state bureaucracy. Neither side wanted to endure that ordeal. The solution was simple and elegant—draft an addendum containing new provisions that superseded the objectionable clauses.

In another negotiation, between a U.S. hotel chain and an Asian government, an impasse was reached when the government refused to allow the payment of a management services fee to the U.S. company of 10 percent of net revenue in U.S. dollars. The Asian country believed it could not spare more than 3 percent to preserve its extremely spare supply of foreign currency. The U.S. hotel chain could not justify becoming involved if it could not remit profits home. By ignoring positions and examining interests, the negotiators were able to reach an agreement in which a 10 percent fee payable in U.S. currency was allowed to be paid provided that the hotel operation generated at least 30 percent of its gross profit in U.S. dollars or other "hard currency." The U.S. company received its royalty and the Asian government ensured a net gain of hard currency.

In some cases interests can be reconciled simply by characterizing facts in different ways. We were recently involved in buy-out negotiations between two partners in a small corporation. One partner, who owned 49 percent of the shares, was negotiating to buy out the 51 percent interest of the company's founder, who wanted to retire. The founder was not particularly sophisticated in financial matters but had an insatiable ego that he was having difficulty separating from the company he had built up. Throughout the negotiations he was adamant that he had to receive a million dollars for his shares. He couldn't justify that figure by any standard formula for valuing a small, closely held company, but it remained a fixation for him. He didn't seem particularly interested in the various deal structures that were being proposed or in the actual economic value of what was being offered him. He kept coming back to the same point: "I don't care how you lawyers and MBA-types structure it, as long as I get my million dollars." It was relatively simple to satisfy the founder's demand by providing for a series of ten payments of $100,000 each over ten years. The numbers were simple and understandable—and they totaled a neat $1 million. The new 100 percent owner was quite happy with the result, since the present value of those payments discounted back with a 10 percent interest rate was only about $675,000. Moreover, he expected to be able to make those payments out of the cash flow of the company, minimizing his financing needs. Each partner got what he wanted out of the deal, which is the essence of successful negotiation.

Yet another case of interests prevailing over positions involved one of the authors negotiating the terms of a major joint-venture agreement between U.S. and Japanese companies. The negotiators had made good progress until they reached the arbitration clause in the agreement. The Japanese side wanted to have any arbitration held in Japan, while our position was that any arbitration take place in the United States. The Japanese were motivated in their insistence in part by nationalistic pride as well as convenience, while the Americans shared convenience as a motive but also believed the process would be more fair and efficient in the United States. As the discussions continued, the Japanese negotiator asked the American whether his company had ever participated in an arbitration. Answering honestly, the American admitted that the situation had never arisen. The Japanese side, feeling that since the

Americans had never arbitrated, and also sensing that neither side would ever want to go to arbitration, suggested the arbitration take place in Hawaii. That way, in the unlikely event an arbitration did take place, everyone could play golf while the dispute was being resolved. With that shared interest identified, agreement was reached.

CREATE AND CLAIM VALUE

The old idea of a good bargain was a transaction in which one man got the better of another. The new contract is a transaction which is good for both parties to it.

—*Justice Louis Brandeis*

To be hard does not mean to be hard as stone and to be soft does not mean to be soft as water.

—*Kikuyu Proverb*

Negotiation actually consists of two distinct processes: creating value and claiming value. Creating value is a cooperative process whereby the parties to the negotiation seek to realize the full potential benefit of the relationship. Without some potential for creating value, there would be no incentive for negotiating. One would voluntarily choose to engage in the interaction only if one believed oneself capable of prevailing on the basis of power or deception. Claiming value, on the other hand, is essentially a competitive process. While it is possible, in a given instance, that the division of benefits from a relationship would flow naturally from the contributions of the parties, usually some element of bargaining is involved whereby one party's gain is the other's loss. The relative importance of the cooperative and competitive elements in any given negotiation will vary. However, the basis of the negotiation must be cooperation. If the competitive element predominates, the basis of the negotiation can be undermined.

The key to **creating** value in a negotiation is finding interests that the parties have in common or that complement each other, and then reconciling and expanding upon these interests. This value-creating process is sometimes referred to as a "win-win" approach to negotiation. A creative win-win approach to negotiation can be illustrated with the classic example of two sisters faced with the prospect of dividing a single orange. Some people would assume that the only solution would be to divide the orange into halves. These same people, presumably lawyers, would then fight over which sister should receive which half in the event the cut of the orange was imprecise. By determining their respective interests, however, the two hypothetical sisters might be able to fashion a distributive compromise, with one sister obtaining the juice she desired and the other sister the peel with which to bake a cake. The key to creating value in this example is not viewing the item being negotiated as a "fixed pie" (to mix metaphors), which, when divided, necessarily produces a loss for any party's gain.

The following six-point approach can help craft cooperative solutions that create a continuing incentive to maintain and enhance the relationship:

1. Separate the issues from the relationship and approach each one separately;
2. Look through positions to find interests;
3. Advance clear objectives that satisfy the interests of each negotiator;
4. Measure solutions against these objectives;
5. Examine the range of possible solutions before staking out positions; and
6. Guard against being stripped of the value that creates continuing mutual interest in maintaining and strengthening the relationship.

One way to discover opportunities to create value is to list all the variables that can be altered in reaching an agreement. Many inexperienced negotiators will focus only on price or some other obvious variable. Even in a simple sales transaction other variables, such as payment terms, delivery, quality, and quantity, usually can be manipulated to produce a creative negotiated result. The world is full of inspirational examples of creative manipulation of available variables. Western companies, constrained in their attempts to sell to Eastern Bloc countries by the lack of hard currency reserves in those countries, have adopted a variety of creative solutions. In 1990, negotiators on behalf of Pepsico concluded agreements to exchange over $3 billion worth of their company's product for a comparable value of vodka and ships built in the Soviet Union. A Canadian company agreed to build nuclear plants in Romania in return for railcars and coal.

Another technique we have found to be valuable in breaking a creative deadlock is to write out your objectives for the negotiation, and that of your counterpart, and all the various assumptions that constrain your range of options. Then, beginning with your objectives and running through all your assumptions, question each. Strip everything down to its basic elements and question them. Constantly ask yourself, Is this really a given or is there some way to change it or get around it? When the breakthrough does occur, it will usually appear obvious. But the method of its revelation may have been a disciplined and methodical questioning of assumptions.

The greater the number of variables, the greater the range of possibilities for creating value for each negotiator. Too often, negotiators fail to utilize third parties in an attempt to reconcile interests. The international Third World debt crisis that began in earnest in 1982 has created nearly continuous negotiations between Western commercial banks and Third World governments. Looking at these disputes as two-party engagements limits possible solutions. As an example, creative negotiators have been able to involve environmental groups in "multilateral circular exchanges" with the banks and debtor governments that have achieved the interests of all parties to the negotiation. In 1987, Conservation International purchased $650,000 in debt owed by Bolivia to a Swiss bank for $.15 on the dollar. Conservation International then agreed to surrender the notes, evidencing the $650,000 to the Bolivian government in return for the designation of nearly 350,000 acres of land as an environmentally protected zone and for resources to manage the zone. In this example, an A versus B situation was resolved by A exchanging with C and C exchanging with B. Similar creative thinking allowed Salomon Brothers to arrange a transaction in which Sweden forgave $24.5 million in debt to Costa Rica in return for that country's agreement to protect 210,000 acres of land by creating a national park.

One of the classic tales of value creation was told by Mark

Twain. The author was sitting in front of a hotel when a dog sat down beside him. A general walked by, caught sight of the dog, and said:

> "He is very fine—he is a wonder; would you sell him?"
>
> I was greatly moved . . . I said, "Yes."
>
> The General said, "What do you ask for him?"
>
> "Three dollars."

The general was most pleased and a bargain was struck. The owner of the dog came looking for his pet. Twain asked whether the man was looking for a dog. The man answered affirmatively. Twain then said:

> "He was here a minute ago, and I saw him follow a gentleman away. I think I could find him for you if you would like me to try."
>
> I have seldom seen a person look so grateful. . . . I said I would do it with great pleasure but that as it might take a little time I hoped he would not mind paying me something for my trouble. He said he would do it most gladly . . . and asked me how much. I said, "Three dollars."
>
> He looked surprised, and said, "Dear me, it is nothing! I will pay you ten, quite willingly."
>
> But I said, "No, three is the price," and I started for the stairs without . . . further argument. . . . When I reached the room, I found the General there caressing his dog, and quite happy. I said, "I am sorry, but I have to take the dog again."
>
> He seemed very much surprised and said, "Take him again? Why, he is my dog; you sold him to me. . . ."
>
> "Yes," I said, "it is true—but I have to have him, because the man . . . that owns him . . . wants him again . . . he wasn't my dog."
>
> The General looked even more surprised. . . . "Do you mean to tell me that you were selling another man's dog—and knew it?"

"Yes, I knew it wasn't my dog. . . . Put yourself in my place. Suppose you had sold a dog that didn't belong to you. . . ."

"Oh," he said, "don't muddle my brains any more. . . . Take him along and give me a rest."

So I paid back the three dollars and led the dog downstairs and passed him over to his owner, and collected three dollars for my trouble.

I went away then with a good conscience, because I had acted honorably; I never could have used the three that I sold the dog for, because it was not rightly my own, but the three I got for restoring him to his rightful owner was righteously and properly mine, because I had earned it.

While there can be a competitive element to negotiation, particularly in determining the division of gains, it is usually counterproductive to think of negotiation as adversarial. Negotiating models built on gamesmanship, in particular, lend themselves to military and sports analogies. Such adversarial models break down on one important point: you can't have a loser in a successful negotiation. If you approach a negotiation with the objective of "defeating" an "opponent," your chances of winning from the process are poor.

An acquaintance of ours, a prominent American CEO, tells the following story to describe the current state of economic competition between Japan and the United States:

Two businessmen, an American and a Japanese, were fishing in the Alaskan wilderness. They were gleefully hauling in salmon the size of basset hounds when a large grizzly bear ambled onto the scene. Both men froze as they found their place in the food chain reversed. Coming to grips with this development, the Japanese businessman began furiously to replace his hip waders with running shoes.

"Do you really think you can outrun a grizzly bear?" the American asked incredulously. The Japanese replied: "I don't need to outrun the bear. I only need to outrun you."

Obviously, this CEO views the relationship between the United States and Japan as being adversarial in nature. In so doing, he may be overlooking valuable areas of cooperation.

The importance of avoiding an adversarial approach was apparent to the authors in a negotiation to end a joint venture in Brazil. It was less apparent to the head of the U.S. company in that venture, whom we will call Scott, as he sought to buy out his Brazilian partner, Francisco. The joint venture had been formed with great optimism, as these joint ventures typically are, five years before the split. The Brazilian company had developed some fairly sophisticated technology, the primary market for which was in the United States. The U.S. company had the capital and marketing presence in the United States that the Brazilian company needed to fully exploit its technology. The two companies, brought together by the personal friendship of their respective principals, formed a joint venture, which they based in Brazil to take advantage of that country's lower labor costs and the personal leadership of Francisco, who was the driving force behind the project.

During the first three years of the venture, its promise increased as the technology proved successful and the potential market in the United States appeared to be greater than at first thought. The value of each company's interest in the venture at that time was probably $10 million to an enthusiastic buyer. The decision to locate the venture in Brazil had been a bad one, however, as labor problems more than offset lower costs, and the venture's distance from the U.S. market and Francisco's personal predilections led it to focus on technical nuances at the expense of marketing considerations. Its location in Brazil also meant that Scott was unable to exercise much control over the venture, and he eventually concluded that he had to buy out Francisco and move the venture to the United States. This decision was a difficult one for Scott, as he and Francisco had been close friends for over twenty years, going back to graduate school at Harvard. That friendship had become strained as the value of the venture eroded. Complicating the situation were Francisco's marital problems, which made it increasingly difficult for him to make the emotional investment required to extricate the venture from its difficulties. He vacillated between extremes in his desire to retain control of the venture. By the time Scott concluded that he had to buy out

Francisco, the financial condition of the venture had become desperate.

Scott's business success was attributable, in part, to his strong competitive nature, and once the issue was engaged he instinctively adopted an adversarial approach to his negotiations with Francisco. Scott was convinced that he could force Francisco out for no more than $1 million. Without a further capital infusion from the United States, the value of the venture would soon be eclipsed by its debts. While neither partner wanted to see their progeny deteriorate to that point, it did offer an opportunity for Scott to exert additional pressure on a nearly broken Francisco.

When Scott proposed this approach to us, we took it under advisement and then advised him to offer no less than $2 million for Francisco's interest. Scott insisted that he could force Francisco out for $1 million. And we agreed. But in so doing, Francisco would be left defeated, and embittered, and the transition of control over the venture would be a traumatic and costly process. The potential value of the venture under the management of the U.S. company was many times greater than what it would cost to negotiate a buy-out that would still allow Francisco to keep his pride and remain actively concerned with the fate of the venture.

Scott agreed, somewhat reluctantly, to follow our approach. Negotiations were difficult because of Francisco's erratic emotional state (and the lack of a buy/sell provision in the original joint-venture agreement, which would have provided a fair and efficient mechanism by which one partner could buy out the other). Scott ended up paying $2.5 million for Francisco's interest, much of which was contingent on the future prosperity of the venture, and Francisco was happy with the deal. The move to the United States went as smoothly as one could hope for under the circumstances, and the venture is now worth several tens of millions of dollars, none of which would have been possible without Francisco's committed involvement. Francisco was greatly relieved to be liberated from the burdens of managing the venture. Scott is enjoying that management, free of partnership hassles, and has become much wealthier in the process. And Scott and Francisco are still close friends.

Every negotiation has both cooperative and competitive components. Adopting either extreme, however, may produce a less than optimal result. Cooperation is required to determine each side's interests and craft an arrangement that maximizes the mutual gain. Competition is usually entailed in determining how mutual gains are to be divided. But if the competition results in unilateral advantage, the basis for cooperation disappears. An overly competitive negotiator may sacrifice the joint gains that can be produced through reciprocal exchange. An overly cooperative negotiator may fail to claim his share of the value created. As is usually the case in human affairs, the ideal is a balance between the extremes.

New information and alternatives should be encountered during the course of an international negotiation if genuine communication is taking place. It is safe to assume that no amount of prior experience in a foreign country could acquaint you with every possible option. This makes it particularly difficult to set a "bottom line" for negotiations in a foreign context. The most advantageous negotiated result can usually be evaluated only as the negotiations progress.

Change in a relationship is inevitable; negotiation is essential to keep this change from destroying the relationship. Since change is a given, the challenge is to make the changes an opportunity to create new value.

The creation of gain in a negotiation can be frustrated if you are not willing to adapt and change positions in response to new information. A Zen master named Zhantang wrote:

> For wayfarers of all times, the right strategy for skillfully spreading the Way essentially lies in adapting. Those who do not know how to adapt stick to the letter and cling to doctrines, get stuck on forms and mired in sentiments—none of them succeed in strategic adaptation. . . . So we know that advanced people who know how to get through counter the ordinary to merge with the Way. They do not fail positively by sticking to one thing.

KNOW YOURSELF AND THE OTHER NEGOTIATOR

Make it thy business to know thyself, which is the most difficult lesson in the world.

—Miguel de Cervantes

Know thyself.

—Inscription at the Delphic Oracle

In order to build a global bridge, you must first recognize the differences between yourself and the other negotiator that need to be spanned. Especially in the international context, these differences are often largely differences in perception. Dealing with these differences in perception requires determining the point from which each negotiator views an issue. Obviously, you need to understand the other negotiator if you are to develop the sense of "connectedness" that is the first step in all constructive communication. Just as important, however, you need to understand your *own* interests, motives, and perceptions.

One useful technique for dealing with differences in perception is to examine the issue being negotiated from the other person's point of view. Imagine yourself in the other negotiator's shoes and think about where the shoes hurt or could fit better. (This may be excruciating if you are negotiating in Asia and have size 11 feet.) Try also to imagine how your counterpart views relationship factors like relative status, power, resources, patience, and character. This new perspective will allow you to more accurately identify the needs, interests, and expectations of the other negotiator.

Just as communication expands the range of options, so shared experience enhances communication. In his book *Gestalt Therapy Verbatim*, Frederick S. Perls writes:

> You speak a certain language, you have certain attitudes, certain behavior and the two worlds somewhere overlap. And in this overlapping area communication is possible.

The skill lies in making the overlapping area as broad as possible. In many cases, this just requires spending time together, doing things together. These activities might have nothing to do with the specific negotiation and yet have everything to do with the negotiation process. It helps to view any negotiation as just one chapter in an ongoing relationship, rather than as a discrete deal. Increase the area of opportunity by increasing your knowledge of each other.

The imperfect nature of any person's information about the deal, uncertainty of any given negotiator's information, and the "wild card" of human emotion each can radically affect a person's perception of a negotiation. The best way to deal with these wild-card variables is through information—as much of it as you can get. But information is only useful to a receptive mind, which means, don't judge. Judgment entails fitting new information into your existing frame of reference. The idea is to expand your frame of reference.

Once you have determined the relative points of view of yourself and your counterpart, you can begin the process of bringing these different perspectives together. The goal of a negotiator is to create a shared perception of a situation. Within this shared perception lies the area of possible agreement.

Changing the perceptions of the other person is the essence of persuasion. One of the most difficult perceptual problems in an international negotiation is the common tendency to **assume** that the other negotiator perceives a situation in a similar manner to yourself. This tendency is called projective cognitive similarity by sociologists (but then, sociologists always have to make a commonsense idea sound like a scientific revelation). In simple terms, people assume that other people have the same needs, values, interests, and goals that they do. What is needed to break this habit of making assumptions is, in effect, a cultural deconditioning process. In the absence of a Betty Ford Center for Ethnocentrism, the key is to become aware of the interaction and of the differences.

There is no shortage of national and cultural stereotypes. Americans are impatient, direct, aggressive, creative, friendly, materialistic, and often tactless. Germans are rigid, hardworking, disciplined, domineering, and well-organized. Asians are inscrutable, reserved, status-conscious, patient negotiators who avoid open conflict and emphasize personal relationships. Latins are romantic, impractical, leisure oriented, disorganized, and obsessed with honor and principle. British negotiators are arrogant, eccentric, reserved, tradition-minded, and fair. Italians are warm, outgoing, emotional, and flirtatious. The Dutch are reliable, direct, serious, honest, and tolerant. Israelis are clever, paranoid, tough, and excellent traders. The Irish are simple, shrewd, argumentative, and fun-loving. The Russians are uncompromising and sentimental. The French are, well, French. The list could go on and on. These stereotypes and prejudices are precisely what caused Emperor Charles V to quip in the 1500s: "I speak Spanish to God, Italian to women, French to men and German to my horse." Cultural bias makes you understand and maybe laugh when you hear the restaurant in heaven defined as a place where the manager is German, the maître d' is French, the waiter is English, and the cook is Italian, while the restaurant in hell has an Italian manager, a German maître d', a French waiter, and an English cook.

These laundry lists of stereotypes are inherently insulting because they dismiss the unique dignity of the individual. Overcoming prejudice and stereotyping, accordingly, entails focusing on the qualities of the individual negotiator rather than on his or her racial and cultural characteristics. Differences within ethnic groups or among countrymen are often far greater than differences between groups.

Recent changes in the Soviet Union provide support for rejecting a stereotyping approach to international dealings. Such an approach to negotiating with the Soviets might lead one to expect a reluctance to compromise, extreme initial positions, emotional bullying, an obsession with gaining or maintaining control, and counterpunching style. But then along comes Mikhail Gorbachev, who has shown a willingness to listen, to compromise, and to take the initiative rather than react.

We have repeatedly made the point that the most effective way to be a better negotiator is to become more aware. Prejudices and stereotypes tend to be applied unconsciously by negotiators. In some cases, subtle unconscious bias can be more damaging to a negotiation than overt bias. Often, simply getting to know the other negotiator can be the best method of eliminating prejudices and stereotypes. In all cases, separate the person from the problem.

When you are negotiating with someone from your own country, it is often possible to expedite communication by making reasonable cultural assumptions. The situation reverses itself when two cultures are involved. As a rule, making assumptions about another culture is counterproductive since it most often leads to misunderstandings and miscommunication. One of the authors has a father who is an identical twin. Family legend says that the two infants could talk to each other in their own language before they knew five words of English. Much of their ability to communicate arose from the totality of their shared experiences. They could assume nearly everything, so communication was simple.

Compare this with a negotiation between an American and a Soviet. Their needs, values, interests, and expectations may differ dramatically. They may have little shared experience. The Soviet and American mentalities have been described by the British botanist Rupert Sheldrake as the yin and yang of cultures. Russia is yin, the female. Russians seek security, the great feminine theme. In Mother Russia, the State provides for all needs. But, like a possessive mother, Russia can smother her children in her captive embrace. The theme of the Great Yang, America, on the other hand, is freedom, the masculine obsession. Americans took a virgin continent by force and went on to lead the world in the subjugation of nature. Following this yin/yang dichotomy, the Cold War was premised on the Russians' fear of the Motherland being violated by the United States, while the Americans feared the smothering of the world by Russia. It is no wonder that U.S.-Soviet negotiations can be difficult. Apply this view of the two cultures, for example, to contract interpretation. The American, emphasizing freedom, will tend to assume that what is not prohibited is permitted. The Soviets, emphasizing the rule of order and security, will tend to assume that what is not permitted is prohibited. Which just goes to show, in international negotiations always question your assumptions.

The propensity of a negotiator to make promises or commitments to another negotiator is directly proportional to his level of trust. Negotiators will not be inclined to exchange commitments if they do not trust that the other will fulfill the commitment. Trust is a measure of the extent to which you believe a negotiator will honor promises, respect limits, obey norms, and protect your interests. Trust must be mutual, and yet one negotiator's level of trust can be higher or lower than his counterpart. Trust is higher when interests are shared or congruent; trust is lower when interests conflict. Trust can also be enhanced through openness and free exchange of information as well as by the depth of experience of the negotiators. Of course, the best way to build trust is to be trustworthy. One becomes trustworthy by showing over time that one can be trusted. Trust can also be developed through communication. But when trust is low, people will be disinclined to communicate honestly—a nasty dilemma, which brings us back to building up trust bit by bit through shared experience.

An acquaintance of ours had the occasion to travel to Addis Ababa, the capital of Ethiopia, in the mid-1980s. After an arduous air journey from Europe, he presented himself at the hotel to which he had been directed by his vigilant travel agent. The hotel had no record of the reservation that the travel agent had allegedly secured. His further research on the subject uncovered the existence of just one vacant room in the hotel. After trudging up the stairs behind the bellman (the elevator, it seems, had found a position in life from which it had no aspirations to rise), he found himself at the door to his room. When the protagonist of our story opened the door, he found nothing but darkness. The bellman shook his head and in halting English asked our traveler to wait. A short time later the bellman returned with a light bulb. Before our traveler could think of a good quip about the number of Ethiopians required to screw in a light bulb, the deed was accomplished. The light revealed four walls, a ceiling, floor, a bare mattress, and nothing more, except a sign on the wall that read in English (and three other languages):

> This room has
>> a light bulb
>> a mattress
>> two sheets
>> a blanket
> Do not steal these properties [*sic*] of the hotel.

When our traveler had absorbed this information, he noticed the bellman smiling broadly, obviously waiting for his tip. "Preposterous," exclaimed our unaccommodating traveler to no one in particular since the bellman's simple grasp of the English language included no word with twelve letters. "No can stay," said our traveler in his best Pidgin English. The bellman and our traveler walked together to the front desk to discuss the condition of the rented room with the desk clerk. "I must have sheets and a blanket," demanded our somewhat agitated traveler. "You will steal," responded the desk clerk, frowning. Our traveler deduced that a basis of trust needed to be established. Out of his pack came four tins of sardines. In short order a deal was arranged. The sardines went into the hotel safe to be kept until the traveler left the hotel with all items on the room inventory accounted for. In due course, our somnolent traveler received sheets and a blanket.

Our traveler's solution to his problem was little different from the American buyer who arrives in the Ivory Coast and delivers a letter of credit to a trader selling cocoa. An item of value has been offered as security if the buyer proves untrustworthy. An exchange has been created that facilitates the trust-building process. There are an infinite number of exchanges that can create trust. (Consider the body parts exchanged by court eunuchs in return for steady employment in comfortable surroundings.) Eventually, if our traveler were to visit the hotel in Addis Ababa many times without stealing, and the cocoa buyer were to make repeated purchases, the security arrangements would become unnecessary. The desk clerk would pony up the bedding sans sardines, and the American could buy the beans without the bond.

Even in the case of adversarial negotiations, it is our experience that a sophisticated counterpart is preferable to an incompetent. It may be possible to outwit or deceive a naive negotiator, but it is more difficult to create value and sustain a productive relationship with such a person. Moreover, the naivete of the other may result in costly miscalculation.

Of course, one shouldn't be misled by expressions of humility. Sam Ervin, the senator from North Carolina who became a media star during the televised Watergate hearings in 1974, often disarmed his adversaries through his folksy, simple style and his self-description as being merely a "country lawyer." The senator failed to mention that he was a Harvard Law School graduate with a razor-sharp mind.

LEARN TO COMMUNICATE

The most immutable barrier in nature is between one man's thoughts and another's.

—*William James*

It is a luxury to be understood.

—*Ralph Waldo Emerson*

We all carry with us into our interactions with others a heavy load of assumptions, biases, myths, experiences, and cultural learning. Variances in these between individuals easily lead to miscommunication. And between individuals from different cultures the variances can be many and extreme. The consequences can be disastrous or merely amusing, often depending merely on whether the variances are recognized and understood.

Even a simple cartoon can reveal a cultural chasm. While practicing law in Tokyo, one of the authors had grown emotionally dependent on the cartoon, *The Far Side*, which appeared every morning in the local English language daily. The lack of any other cartoon in the paper gave this particular feature an almost religious significance among those expatriates who had come to rely on humor to survive and even prosper within the absurd cultural juxtaposition that characterizes modern Tokyo. A particularly good *Far Side* might even lead off the casual banter among the expatriates on the day of its appearance, much as a Super Bowl or World Cup outcome might in their native lands. The morning *Far Side* ritual had become a personal bond among the expatriate lawyers in this particular firm, as it was a point of distinction from their Japanese colleagues. The Japanese lawyers never quite seemed to grasp the subtleties of this idiosyncratic humor. Many of the expatriate lawyers just wrote this lack of appreciation off as a by-product of Japanese cultural inhibition.

One morning two of the expatriate lawyers were indulging in a *Far Side* panel showing a fireman delivering a cat, which he had just retrieved from a tree, to a dog disguised by a mask and overcoat as an old woman. The fireman is saying to the dog, whose tail is wagging enthusiastically, "Now calm down there ma'am. . . . Your cat's gonna be just fine . . . just fine." To the young Americans on this particular morning, it seemed to be one of the funniest situations ever contrived. A Japanese colleague looking over their shoulders expressed his complete lack of empathy. In the heat of the moment, it just didn't seem possible to the Americans that the Asian advocate, whom they knew to possess a sense of humor, could not grasp the manifest genius of this work of popular art. As they undertook to diagnose what appeared to be pathological solemnity on the part of their friend, a couple of critical cultural misunderstandings were revealed.

"What's so funny about a fireman getting a cat down out of a tree?" the Japanese jurist asked.

"Nothing," he was told. "That's not the joke."

"Then why is he doing it?" the dialogue continued.

"Because firemen always get cats down out of trees."

"They do?"

"In the cultural mythology of America they do."

"Well, in Japan they put out fires."

"Ah, so. We have discovered the source of the misunderstanding," one of the Americans deduced. "So now surely you can appreciate the brilliant absurdity of the noble fireman delivering the rescued cat into the clutches of its nemesis."

"Nemesis? Doesn't that mean enemy?" the Japanese lawyer asked, obviously still not appreciating the situation.

"Yeah, basically. You know, fighting like cats and dogs, and all that." This was proving difficult.

"No, I don't know. In Japan cats and dogs get along just fine. Now cats and mice, that's another story, as you say." A second cultural misunderstanding had revealed itself.

"Well, maybe they don't always fight, but in the United States we take it as a general rule that the social relations between these two species are strained. Given that, you must admit it's a pretty darned funny cartoon."

"Not really," the Japanese lawyer concluded.

And by that time, of course, the Americans had to admit that perhaps the cartoon wasn't quite as funny as it had seemed to them at first impression.

The first step in building any relationship is learning how to communicate effectively. Truly effective communication is highly positive (constructive) and has little negative (derailing) content. Communicating effectively, like negotiating, is a skill that must be learned. Various studies floating around claim that the typical American executive spends nearly 80 percent of his or her working day communicating. These voyeuristic researchers also conclude that over 60 percent of executives' time is spent listening and that this listening occurs at only a 25 percent level of efficiency. These findings do not make one sanguine about the efficiency of communication even between people who speak the same language and share a common culture. It's not likely that the efficiency of communication in international dealings is better. Communicating effectively in either a domestic or international context requires that our message be understood and that we listen to the other person.

Most communication problems arise because a person can choose whether to be aware of information and can choose whether to process information rationally (or at least can elect *not* to do either). A person's capacity to be "selectively aware" and "'not to think" allows one to avoid what is or may be unpleasant. Unfortunately, these capacities can also serve as barriers to effective communication. The more you can learn to be fully aware of the information being conveyed and to process the information rationally without emotional interference, the better your communication with another person will be.

Successfully communicating with a person who does not speak English is rewarding in and of itself. Many of us have been in situations where we were confronted with a problem or obstacle and the solution depended on our ability to communicate with a person who spoke no English. Imagine yourself in the French Alps in the winter. Your car battery is dead. You attempt to procure jumper cables from the proprietor of a ski lodge. You try some English words. A number of gestures only succeed in offending the temperamental Frenchman. You are frustrated and so is he. But then you spot a pad and pen and quickly render an infantile drawing of two batteries, each with positive and negative symbols and crudely drawn wires with clamps on each end. He smiles knowingly and you beam. He helps you start your car, shares some red wine, and over-charges you for both. You feel great, not only because of the wine and your ignorance of exchange rates, but because you have successfully communicated. Some of this positive energy occurs every time we connect with another person in this way.

BRIDGE THE LANGUAGE GAP

To work through an interpreter is like hacking one's way through a forest with a feather.

—*James Evans*

Fortunately for Americans, English has clearly emerged as the common language of this global community. As much as business executives from non-English-speaking countries may hate to admit it, English is the linguistic currency of international commerce. The language of business, which may be more accurately described as "broken English" or "English spoken badly," is a legacy of British, then American cultural imperialism. When a German investor, a Korean contractor, a Japanese banker, and an Italian engineer negotiate to build a production facility in Africa for a new consumer electronic product, the negotiation and the documentation will inevitably be in English, even though it is not the native language of any party involved. This example is not hypothetical. Sometimes this international language can even transmute beyond the comprehension of a native English speaker.

One of the authors was drawn into a major negotiation between Japanese and Soviet concerns. Their only common language was English and the author was called upon to set forth the agreement of the parties in an English language contract. As a model for the contract, he was given copies of previous agreements between the same parties. Key provisions of those agreements consisted of meaningless sentence fragments and other gibberish. When he attempted to redraft those provisions in a coherent and comprehensible form, both the Soviets and Japanese reacted with alarm. "Please don't touch those sections," they pleaded. "The language is agreed upon and has formed the basis of all our agreements." (The problem was dealt with by leaving the model provisions intact, but clarifying the points elsewhere in the contract.)

Some Americans defy their national malady and have actually learned one or more foreign languages. However, one's command of a foreign language must be quite advanced to be effective for any purpose other than informal social interaction. What you believe to be passable Arabic may be babble to an Arab. Mark Twain told the following story illustrating this point in his classic travel book, *A Tramp Abroad*:

> When we got down town I found that we could go by rail to within five miles of Heilbronn. The train was just starting, so we jumped aboard and went tearing away in splendid spirits. . . . There were some nice German people in our compartment. I got to talking about some pretty private matters presently, and Harris became nervous; so he nudged me and said:
> "Speak in German—these Germans may understand English."
> I did so, and it was well I did; for it turned out there was not a German in the party who did not understand English perfectly. It is curious how widespread our language is in Germany. After a while some of those folks got out and a German gentleman and his two young daughters got in. I spoke German to one of the latter several times, but without result. Finally she said:
> "Ich verstehe nur Deutsch und Englisch"—or words to that effect. That is, "I don't understand any language but German and English."

Companies from countries all over the world are beginning to use English as their "official" corporate language. One of the first companies to take this step was Philips, the Dutch electronics company. Since 1983 corporate employees of Philips have used English in communicating. When the Swiss company Brown Boveri combined with the Swedish company Asea in 1987 to form ABB, English again was adopted as the official corporate language. Even the linguistically chauvinistic French have made this change in many cases. The French-owned company Carnaud switched its corporate language to English in late 1988. Many more companies around the globe have already made this move on a de facto basis. The move to English as a global standard is being accelerated by the fact that 80 percent of all data in computers is stored in English.

The secret of communicating effectively with a person who uses English as a second language lies in using simple and direct language. When meeting face-to-face with foreign negotiators, speak slowly and repeat yourself often. Avoid using slang and obscure idioms. Contrary to the belief of many Americans, raising your voice does **not** increase the foreigner's comprehension of English. Likewise, speaking at a snail's pace accomplishes nothing if the foreigner speaks no English. A friend of ours witnessed a judge explaining to a Haitian refugee that "sleeping . . . in . . . a . . . public . . . building . . . is . . . illegal." The judge may as well have been speaking a Chinese dialect. Remember also that the ability of a person to write in English is typically much better than his ability to use English in a conversational setting. Moreover, his ability to speak in English is generally better than his ability to listen in English. To compensate for this discrepancy, make your proposals in writing whenever possible and send written summaries of all meetings to the foreign negotiator. Sending a written proposal in advance of a meeting allows your foreign counterpart time before the meeting to review and comprehend the points to be discussed.

The transmission of information, as opposed to achieving understanding and agreement, is best accomplished when the negotiators are not actually meeting. Face-to-face communication is more effectively used for clarifying and supplementing information that has already been transmitted and assimilated. The emotional dynamics of a face-to-face meeting tend to limit a person's ability to transmit and assimilate information. Moreover, each person has a limited ability to hold data in his short-term memory. Research by the Nobel Laureate Herbert Simon has shown that the average person's short-term memory can hold only six to seven pieces of data.

Of course, not everyone speaks English. In such a situation, the use of an interpreter or translator becomes essential. A good interpreter or translator can be worth his or her weight in gold (depending on the current price of gold and the metabolism of the linguist). Effective interpretation requires more than just the ability to speak two languages fluently. A good interpreter will be sensitive to cultural differences and more importantly be capable of exercising judgment in a number of areas. A well-trained interpreter will also know when to paraphrase and when to precisely determine what is being said. An effective interpreter will also pick up verbal and nonverbal cues given by both sides. The interpreter can act as a screen to buffer your mistakes if you say something that is awkward or insulting. A well-trained and intelligent interpreter can be a rare commodity. Some interpreters have even become famous in their own right. The character Honey in Garry Trudeau's comic strip is based on one of the best interpreters in the People's Republic of China.

U.S. federal prosecutors found out the hard way that confirming the qualifications of an interpreter is essential. In the infamous "pizza connection" money laundering case, the U.S. government paid over $170,000 to a Sicilian-English interpreter over three years. This interpreter later testified that although he had worked for the federal government for twenty-five years, he had never studied the Sicilian language, that his expertise came from conversing with a chauffeur on a trip in northern Italy. He admitted that he could not write Sicilian and that he was "not that great when it comes to vocabulary." Even small, seemingly trivial, errors in interpretation can have severe adverse consequences. The phrase "Man, I don't even have ten cents" was interpreted in a trial as "Man, I don't even have ten kilos." Obviously, a major difference. Enough for a mistrial when the mistake was discovered.

In dealing with intercultural communication problems, the difference between interpretation and translation should be noted. An interpreter must listen to what is being said and then quickly or even simultaneously decide how to convey the message in another language. The interpretation process is imprecise at best. While a translator also works with two languages, he has substantially more time to reflect on the proper words to utilize. A translator is able to consult a dictionary or other experts, while an interpreter must work from memory. For this reason, language interpretation is much less accurate than language translation.

Making both interpretation and translation more difficult is the fact that few language experts will have technical expertise in the particular area you are discussing. An American who has studied medieval German literature for many years and who holds himself out to be an interpreter will not necessarily be able to accurately convey technical discussions about chemical formulas. Both translators and interpreters will have great difficulty conveying a meaning that has no equivalent in any other culture. Iamblichus wrotes in *De Mysteriis*: "It is by no means the case that translated terms preserve the original concept; indeed, every nation has some idiomatic expressions that are impossible to render perfectly in the language of another."

The phrase "out of sight, out of mind" was once translated into Russian and back to English as "invisible maniac." Back around the turn of the century, when Western missionaries were swarming around the heathen Japanese like flies going at a piece of rancid meat, some earnest proselytizer translated into Japanese a standard Protestant hymn that included the line, "Throw out a lifeline, thine brother to save." Sometime later the same hymn happened to be translated back into English as, "Fling out a very strong rope made of hemp, the honorable other son of thy venerable parents to rescue." A relatively experienced Soviet once translated "the spirit is willing but the flesh is weak" into "the whiskey is agreeable but the meat has gone bad." In his book *More Like Us*, James Fallows aptly describes how the same words can have very different meanings in multiple cultural contexts:

> The adage "a rolling stone gathers no moss" is taken by the British to be a warning: a British dictionary interprets it, "one who constantly changes his place of employment will not grow rich." To the Japanese its meaning is equally clear: a Japanese specialist in English wrote, "This is obviously a proverb warning against lack of perseverance." But he had to go on to advise his readers that Americans read the proverb differently: "If you keep on moving and being active you will not get rusty."

One well-publicized example of official misinterpretation occurred when U.S. President Jimmy Carter visited Poland in 1977. The interpreter was reported to be a leading figure in his linguistic field. Unfortunately, President Carter's remarks were translated with far less accuracy than the U.S. government typically demands. Upon the President's arrival, the Poles were informed that Carter had "left America never to return." On another occasion President Carter's "desires for the future" were translated as his "lusts for the future." (This latter error may be forgiven by the prominence that President Carter's lusts had received during the presidential campaign the year before.) After Carter's departure, a leading Polish official commented on the performance of the interpreter: "I had to grit my teeth from time to time. But one must not be rude to ladies or interpreters."

Using an interpreter can put you at a significant disadvantage if the foreign negotiator is only pretending not to understand English. This negotiating tactic can achieve a number of objectives. During a negotiation in the Soviet Union, an American company encountered a government official who falsely claimed to speak only Russian. An interpreter was provided by the American company and the negotiations began. When the American spoke, the Soviet official had more than twice the usual time to prepare a response or to formulate a question. The Soviet official was also able to move the negotiations to his benefit by claiming "not to understand" arguments favorable to the American company or by "clarifying" his own translated comments when they did not elicit the desired response from the American. Needless to say, the negotiations went poorly for the Americans and well for the Soviets. After an agreement was signed, a dinner was arranged in a Moscow hotel. The interpreters were performing their usual role when a waiter's tray began to lose a dish loaded with food. The president of the American company was directly below the tray and in a moment would be covered with food. The supposedly monolingual Soviet official exclaimed in perfect English, "Look out!" The Soviet official's reflexive action revealed his deception. The American thanked his Soviet counterpart for the warning and knew better the next time.

Both of the authors have encountered this "I don't speak English" facade in their dealings, at times practiced by their own clients. One of the authors negotiated for two weeks with a Japanese executive who never once revealed to the Americans negotiating opposite him that he had any working knowledge of English. All discussions, formal and informal, went through an interpreter. In fact, the Japanese executive had lived for fifteen years in New York, and spoke flawless English.

At one time, the French language was the accepted medium of expression in diplomacy. For this reason, and because they take such pride in their language, the French are often reluctant to negotiate in English without an interpreter. This phenomenon can be observed in both diplomacy and business. In President Nixon's book *Leaders*, he writes that General de Gaulle "recognized that there was a tactical advantage to conducting his half of the conversation in French. By waiting for the translations of my statements and questions, he doubled the time he had to contemplate his responses. He obviously had this in mind because he listened just as carefully to my original statements as to the translations."

Providing your interpreter with as much assistance as possible is always beneficial. Assisting an interpreter can be accomplished in several ways. First, speak slowly and one sentence at a time. The pause between sentences allows the interpreter time to do his or her job. Some Americans will speak one phrase at a time in an effort to be especially helpful. This can work in some languages, but not in others. Languages where the subject precedes the verb (such as Chinese, Korean, and Japanese) prevent an interpreter from working effectively until the entire sentence is spoken. For this reason, stick to speaking in one sentence intervals.

Second, repeat yourself often so you can be assured that your meaning has been conveyed accurately. When repeating statements, you should try to make the same point by using different words and grammar or by using an entirely different approach. Metaphors can also be helpful at times but require great care. Try to avoid obscure idioms. "I'm tickled to death to be here" was translated into Indonesian as, "This poor man scratched himself until he nearly died only to be with you."

Third, you should have another person listening to the conversation who can speak both languages. Even if this second person's language skills are only fair, he or she can serve as a back-up listener who can identify when the parties are not communicating effectively. This approach may at first sound like an unnecessary expense. Try it once. You may be amazed at the contribution of the back-up listener.

Fourth, be extremely careful when conveying numbers through an interpreter. It is a good idea to write any figures on paper and give them to the other negotiators to assure mutual understanding. Even the British have a different concept of the term *one billion* from Americans. (The United States and Britain are, after all, two countries separated by a common language.)

Fifth, spend some time with the interpreter before the negotiations begin to give him or her as much advance knowledge of the material to be translated as possible. You should provide the interpreter with any relevant written materials and fully explain any technical information.

Finally, give the interpreter rest breaks during long negotiating sessions. Working in two languages is stressful and tiring. Be watchful for signs that your interpreter is becoming tired. You may want to use your back-up interpreter if the primary interpreter becomes too exhausted to be effective.

As a rule, using humor in an international negotiation is not a good idea given the risk of offense or misunderstanding. Virginia Woolf once wrote, "Humor is the first of the gifts to perish in a foreign tongue." The use of humor is most dangerous when the purpose of the joke is merely to make someone laugh or because American protocol seems to require that a speech begin with a funny story. (In Japan, speeches tend to begin with an apology. When giving a speech in Japan, we make it a practice to begin by apologizing for our somewhat weak humor.)

One particularly inappropriate use of humor occurred at a political conference in Seattle. In front of a largely foreign audience, Fred M. Zeder II, the head of the U.S. Overseas Private Investment Corporation, began his keynote address with a joke in which China's late Chairman Mao Zedong is asked by a foreign journalist what "might have happened if Lee Harvey Oswald had assassinated Khrushchev rather than President Kennedy." Mimicking a Chinese accent, Mr. Zeder recounted Mao's reply: "Only one thing certain. Aristotle Onassis would not have married Mrs. Khrushchev." Few listeners were amused. Another questionable example of the use of humor in an intercultural context involved President Bush's envoy to Italy. He is reported to have joked in public after his appointment. "I saw the new Italian Navy. Its boats have glass bottoms so they can see the old Italian Navy." As it turned out, the only thing that sank was the joke.

A well-timed joke can be useful in diffusing tension. To avoid the inherent risk, it is a good idea to use self-deprecating humor. A senior executive at a U.S. hotel company tells the following story:

> During a recent negotiation in Tokyo, a bright and witty senior executive of a Japanese company took a stand on an item that was really rather unimportant to his company. After we discussed the item for an extended period of time, I asked him why this item was important to him. After thinking for some time, he replied, "Because we lost the war." We all laughed and went on to another issue. His timing was great.

The most probable risk in telling a joke is that your foreign audience will not understand the humor. An incident involving the character Honey of the *Doonesbury* comic strip illustrates the difficulty of translating humor, as well as the dexterity of a skilled interpreter in bridging the cultural gap. In the first frame of the cartoon, Honey interprets the words of the character Duke and adds at the end, "I think he's about to tell a joke." Duke tells his humorous story and then waits for a response. Rather than trying to retell the joke, Honey says, "The joke has been made, and he will be expecting you to laugh at it. Go wild."

Despite the fact that language translation is easier than language interpretation, you must also be careful to ensure that the proper message is being conveyed by a translator. Many companies have learned this lesson the hard way. Words are not always what they seem. It took weeks for a manufacturer in Singapore to determine that an order for 100,000 trombones from the U.S. military in Vietnam was an order for paper clips.

Doonesbury
BY GARRY TRUDEAU

Trombone is the French word for this simple fastening device. One can only imagine the reaction of the Vietcong to a rendition of "101 Trombones in the Big Parade" played by 100,000 U.S. infantrymen. An American soft drink company discovered that the name of its product had been translated into Chinese to mean "female horse fattened with wax." A manufacturer of oil service equipment provided an unintended lesson in American marketing practices at a trade show in the Soviet Union by displaying a banner that declared the products would improve the user's sex life. "Come Alive With Pepsi," when translated improperly into German proclaimed that the soft drink would help you return from the grave.

LISTEN

Nobody ever listened himself out of a job.

—*Calvin Coolidge*

We have been given two ears and but a single mouth in order that we may hear more and talk less.

—*Zeno of Citium*

Listening is such an important part of communication that it is worthy of separate treatment in this book. Americans are, as a rule, good at arguing but terrible at listening. Dean Rusk, one of America's most experienced international negotiators, said, "One of the best ways to persuade others is with your ears—by listening." The next time you speak or negotiate with someone, check to see whether you are more concerned with your response than with what the other person is trying to communicate. You are likely to find that you are preoccupied with conveying rather than receiving information.

To listen properly to another negotiator, you should work to exclude your subjective opinions, preconceptions and emotional filters. By receiving the information unfiltered, you can truly know the other negotiator and more effectively determine her interests and motives. Most people receive information as if it were an echo of their own perceptions. Instead, accept the negotiator "as he is" and focus on the message. This does not require agreeing to the proposition being advanced. Your intent should be to understand the other negotiator so you can investigate possibilities for crafting a mutually satisfactory agreement.

We tend to be particularly inept at listening to people from another culture, since the message comes cloaked in all manner of assumptions and biases. An incident illustrating this point occurred in Kenya to an American taking a bus from Mount Kilimanjaro to the coast. The bus was filled to capacity with the resident population and all manner of animate and inanimate cargo. The white-skinned American was a stark contrast to the other occupants. After about an hour's drive, the bus stopped and an elderly African woman struggled on board with a load of bundles that seemed to dwarf her own mass. The American, who had lived in Kenya for ten years, said in near perfect Swahili, "Would you like my seat?" The woman stared back at the American and said nothing. The question was repeated, and again the woman said nothing. The woman turned to another Kenyan and said in Swahili, "Can you believe this white man expects me to understand his English?" Variations of this incident have been repeated to the authors from a number of different regions of the world. People who are not really listening see or hear what they expect to see or hear, not what actually exists. Napoleon Bonaparte wrote: "The unforgivable sin of a commander is to 'form a picture'—to assume that the enemy will act a certain way in a given situation, when in fact his response may be altogether different." To avoid this problem, don't assume or presume. Try to listen objectively.

Because they tend not to listen aggressively, Americans may be inclined to spend large amounts of time formulating and conveying arguments to capture some element of value that their foreign counterparts never wanted. In listening to the other negotiator, the key to maximizing efficiency is to concentrate on the message. Our ability to concentrate is often limited by the fact that our minds can think at four to five times the rate we speak.

Listening is such an important skill that experienced international negotiators often bring someone to the negotiation whose sole function is to listen and take detailed notes on each session. After each meeting and during breaks the other negotiators are then briefed by the designated listener. Try using this designated listener approach. You may be surprised to learn how much information you miss.

Other techniques for improving listening skills include:

1. Wait until the entire message is given before responding. Try not to interrupt. Focus on the message and resist the temptation to refute arguments until after you have fully received the information. Don't stop listening too soon.
2. Avoid distractions, since they lower the level of concen-

tration of both the speaker and the listener. Be aware of particular situations that tend to be distracting. Listening skills tend to drop significantly, when you are digesting a large lunch, for example, on a hot afternoon.

3. Don't make assumptions. Don't be judgmental or show disapproval either verbally or nonverbally while the other person is speaking.

4. Focus on the message being transmitted and not the words being utilized. Don't focus on illogical points in a speaker's presentation or inept verbal presentation skills. Work at receiving the information and not at critiquing the speaker.

5. Ask open-ended questions that allow the speaker to elaborate on his response.

6. Take notes of key points. Do not take verbatim notes as you will miss much of the message. If you need complete notes, assign another person specifically to this task.

7. To improve your ability to use what you hear, take the time after the negotiation to write down what each negotiator said and how they said it. Do it as soon as possible before you are distracted by subsequent events. Short-term memory fades fast.

8. Focus your attention on the present moment. Try to block out the future and the past and concentrate on the here and now. By doing this, you can block out irrelevant issues as well as deal objectively with the message being conveyed.

Listening is important in all negotiations, but its importance is heightened in international negotiations, where communication may be hindered by cultural and linguistic differences. The subtleties of indirect communications may be lost without shared context. A great deal of attention should be given to context and nonverbal communication to accurately understand your foreign counterparts.

Words are not always what they appear to be. The context in which words are spoken can entirely alter their meaning.

Context can be defined as situational and cultural factors affecting communication, including the nature of relationships, the environment, the roles of the participants, and nonverbal communication. The greater the contextual portion of communication in any given culture, the more difficult it will be for you to convey or receive a message. Conversely, it is easier to communicate with a person from a culture in which context contributes relatively little to a message. Countries can be thought of as ranging on a continuum from high context to low context, with the East Asian countries on the high context end and the Germanic countries on the low context end.

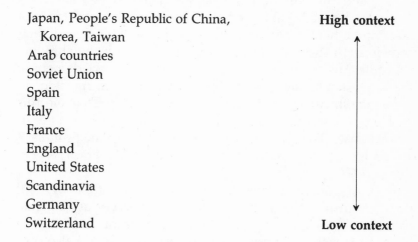

Japan, People's Republic of China,   **High context**
   Korea, Taiwan
Arab countries
Soviet Union
Spain
Italy
France
England
United States
Scandinavia
Germany
Switzerland   **Low context**

This high-to-low-context continuum can be useful for spotting tendencies, but it shouldn't cause one to engage in stereotyping or unconscious negotiating behavior.

Diplomat Raymond Smith makes note of contextual differences in his book *Negotiating with the Soviets*:

> We Americans tend to be low context people. We focus on the substantive issues, on what is being said: "Just the facts, ma'am." The Soviets are considerably higher context. Issues involving authority, risk and control, and how they affect the relationship among the negotiating parties, are so important to them that it may be difficult for them to get to the subjects on the agenda until those issues are resolved.

Contextual communication problems often arise when Americans do business in Japan, a highly contextual culture. Japanese negotiators tend to be reluctant to answer a question with a negative response. "No" in Japanese is often expressed as, "a little difficult," or even just, "a little . . . " preceded by an inward sucking of air through the teeth. "Yes," on the other hand, may only mean that the Japanese is acknowledging that he has heard what you said. We are familiar with one case where an American executive made the following request to his Japanese supplier: "I need you to ship five containers of printers within two weeks." The Japanese supplier answered "yes," and the American left Japan. Three weeks later, the American learned that the printers had not left Japan. He later discovered that the Japanese executive knew at the time of their conversation that he would not be able to meet the shipping schedule. His answer of "yes" was just an acknowledgment of the request. His Japanese upbringing made him reluctant to raise the difficulties entailed in such a schedule. To avoid this problem, ask questions that do not lend themselves to a yes or no response. "When is the earliest you can ship the printers?" would have been a better question from the American executive.

When negotiating, Japanese executives will often say, "I'll think about it." This is often a literal translation of "kangete okimasu." This Japanese phrase usually is meant to convey the message that the proposal is impossible. You should also consider this cultural variation when you inform Japanese or other Asian negotiators that you "will think about it," since they may assume you have given a negative answer.

Another contextual problem arises in Asia because of the difference between formal surface relations and the reality of the relationship. The Japanese call this a dichotomy between *tatemae* (literally, facade) and *honne* (one's real intent). In our experience, Japanese tend to be meticulous about complying with an agreement that is clearly understood but will take advantage of ambiguity in the agreement to their favor. To avoid problems in a highly contextual culture, probe the surface of communication and relationships to find the underlying substance. Make sure the agreement is clear.

A good negotiator listens both with his ears and with his eyes. Among those who have studied nonverbal communication was Sigmund Freud, who wrote:

> He that has eyes to see and ears to hear may convince himself that no mortal can keep a secret. If his lips are silent, he chatters with his fingertips; betrayal oozes out of him at every pore.

Nonverbal communication can take many forms, including tone of voice, body and facial gestures, spatial distances, and dress. During the Cuban missile crisis, Kennedy and Khrushchev communicated nonverbally through military posturing. The movement of ships and missiles was the principal way the two men communicated. Nonverbal messages tend to have more credibility than verbal messages, as they are less likely to be the subject of intentional distortion. Consequently, when a conflict exists between verbal and nonverbal messages, the latter tend to be given greater weight.

Nonverbal communication styles vary significantly between cultures, which can be a source of misunderstanding. Japanese negotiators may consider avoiding direct eye contact an appropriate gesture of humility, whereas an American may have difficulty trusting a person who refuses to look him in the eye. In Bulgaria, nodding your head means "no," and shaking your head, "yes." A "thumbs up" gesture is considered vulgar in Iran and some places in Africa but is common and friendly in Brazil. Folding your arms may be considered disrespectful by a Fijian. Pointing at something with a finger is considered rude in many places in Africa. In Greece waving may be taken as an insult. An "A-OK" gesture considered perfectly appropriate by an American is likely to be viewed as obscene by a Brazilian. The list of potential nonverbal faux pas is nearly endless. If you do make an innocent or unintentional mistake, be easy on yourself. Presumably, you are only human. But in the same spirit, do not be quick to judge the behavior of your foreign counterpart.

As a rule, it is a good idea to simplify your actions and gestures, while still being yourself. This minimizes the risk that your gestures are contradicting your words.

MAINTAIN CONTACT

Distance has the same effect on the mind as on the eye.

—Samuel Johnson

You cannot shave a man's head in his absence.

—Nigerian Proverb

A strong ongoing relationship is best incubated and sustained through numerous and prolonged contacts with your foreign counterpart. Constructive communication requires that the negotiators maintain continual engagement. Personal contact is the most effective method of fostering the relationship. During crucial negotiations with a group of hostile Palestinians, Israeli Prime Minister Golda Meir insisted on meeting her opponents face to face. During an interview, a journalist questioned why such a meeting was necessary. "Even divorces are arranged without personal confrontation," he argued. "I'm not interested in a divorce," responded Mrs. Meir. "I'm interested in a marriage."

Regular consultations and meetings can be particularly important in multiparty negotiations. We were involved in one such negotiation where, after a long period of intense negotiations, a break in meetings was necessary until certain technical data and governmental approvals could be obtained. Not too long after the last meeting, rumors began to circulate about secret negotiations between some of the participants in the negotiation. The absence of regular contact between the negotiators caused a breakdown in the trust that had been built up between the parties. We found that the only way to restore this trust was to reinitiate face-to-face contacts among all concerned.

People pay more attention to matters that are immediate and tangible. Because international negotiations can involve great distances, business relationships can atrophy through neglect. Once you or your foreign counterpart returns home, progress toward reaching agreement nearly always slows to a crawl or even ceases entirely. Communicating by telephone, telex, or facsimile is no substitute for personal contact. This means that despite the expense involved, making regular trips to the foreign country may be necessary if the relationship is to develop. Meetings create deadlines as well as the expectation of progress. People work and devote attention to a matter simply because you have traveled to meet with them. As a rule, the longer you have traveled, the more the other negotiator will feel compelled to devote time and resources to preparation.

Maintaining progress in a negotiation or improving the quality of a global bridge can be greatly facilitated by stationing one or more individuals in the foreign country. Sending an employee abroad will inevitably involve a considerable expense, but can be vital to the success of the business venture. This employee can serve as a conduit or "hot line" over which information can flow to both prevent and resolve disputes. The resident employee is also a tangible symbol of one's commitment to the relationship.

3

Winning Strategies and Tactics in International Negotiations

PREPARATION

In all negotiations of difficulty, a man may not look to sow and reap at once; but must prepare business, and so ripen it by degrees.

—*Francis Bacon*

A man prepared has fought half the battle.

—*Don Quixote*

We can't cross a bridge until we come to it; but I always like to lay down a pontoon ahead of time.

—*Bernard Baruch*

Negotiators can be forgiven for making mistakes, but there is no excuse for being unprepared. Preparation is essential if one is to take the initiative rather than react to events. Counterpunching only works when you are prepared before the first punch is thrown. Meetings tend to fail in inverse proportion to the time spent in preparation and in direct proportion to the time spent meeting. The attention span of the average person in a meeting falls substantially after about one hour. Ironically, you make a meeting shorter by preparing more.

During the preparation stage, assemble as much information relevant to the negotiation as is practically possible. This information can be obtained from third parties and from the other negotiator. The information needed to properly plan for a negotiation may not be easy or inexpensive to obtain. In many cases you will need to rely upon estimates, rather than hard data. Nevertheless, a plan based on estimates is superior to no plan at all.

When you are collecting information, a good starting point is the six basic questions identified in Rudyard Kipling's famous lines:

> I keep six honest serving men,
> They taught me all I know,
> Their names are What?,
> and Why? and When,
> and How? and Where? and Who?

This simple wisdom may be adapted to information gathering in negotiation by a few more specific queries:

1. What is the nature of the matter being negotiated?
2. What are the interests of the respective parties?
3. What resources are available for finding a mutually satisfactory result?
4. Who should be involved in the negotiations?
5. Who are the decision makers?
6. Where should the negotiations take place?
7. When should negotiating sessions take place?
8. How will the negotiated agreement affect parties involved in the negotiation and third parties?

As stated earlier, it is important to make explicit all your assumptions, and then question each. Know which variables are subject to manipulation, and look for ways to change or get around those that at first inspection appear to be immutable.

All the clever strategies and tactics cannot substitute for thorough preparation and a clear focus on the interests you hope to advance and reconcile through the negotiations.

Develop a Flexible Negotiating Plan

A wise man adapts himself to circumstances as water shapes itself to the jar that contains it.

—Chinese Proverb

After the necessary information has been gathered, strategy and tactics should be developed for the other stages of the negotiation. Before each negotiating session, you should have identified the issues that might be raised. As part of your preparation for a negotiating session, create a written negotiating plan. This negotiating plan should contain the following information:

1. Your interests in the negotiation;
2. An estimate of the other party's interests in the negotiation;
3. Your initially desired outcome (in other words, an initial sense of the outcome you seek, while not constraining the possibilities for creating value);
4. An estimate of the other party's initially desired outcome;
5. Possible conflicts or disparities between the parties' initially desired outcomes (that is, where you are likely to get hung up and where creative reconciliation of interests is required);
6. The abilities and limitations of the respective parties in relation to the range of possible outcomes;
7. Additional information you require; and
8. Additional information required by the other party.

In establishing your negotiating plan, be sure to identify the issues that are most important and establish objectives and priorities. Set both objectives and priorities in terms of interests, not necessarily specific outcomes. Unless you can distinguish in advance what your most important interests are, you can't direct the course of the negotiation toward their achievement. You should assume that your foreign counterpart will also be well prepared and will ask penetrating questions with regard to your company, products, and industry. Have the relevant information at hand and be prepared for exhaustive discussions. Investigate the foreign company's business, markets, financial status, and reputation prior to your first meeting. It can also be helpful to thoroughly research current economic conditions and government policies in the foreign country, as these can help illuminate the interests of your foreign counterpart and reveal opportunities for creative problem solving.

A good negotiating plan will be revised continually to reflect new information and ideas as the negotiation progresses. If it isn't, you are probably not listening and learning. Effective negotiation is a process of creative collaboration. During the course of any negotiation, economic conditions, as well as the needs and goals of the negotiators, can change, partly by circumstance and partly by design. You should be sensitive to these changes and be flexible in adapting to them.

Confucius once said: "The superior man does not set his mind either for anything or against anything." Coach Vince Lombardi of the Green Bay Packers, legendary for his methodical devotion to planning and preparation, nonetheless recognized the importance of a quarterback's being free to call an "audible" to revise the play at the last minute. Lombardi once defined life as "a whole series of audibles." When you are approaching a negotiation, it is wise to remember James Russell Lowell's admonition that "only the foolish and the dead never change their opinions."

Control the Agenda

A ship that hath no rudder must have a rock.

—*Italian Proverb*

If you are going to achieve your objectives in a negotiation, you need to know what you want and make sure that the negotiations stay focused on it. From a procedural standpoint, this requires that you develop an agenda and strive to get it adopted. The agenda and other procedural points are as much a part of the negotiating process as are substantive issues. By definition, the agenda and other procedural aspects of a negotiation are negotiable. An agenda is often nothing more than a brief outline of the negotiating session. A properly constructed agenda is a schematic map of the negotiation process. In many of the most productive negotiations in which the authors have been involved, both parties participated in setting the agenda. This means making joint decisions about the agenda—negotiating about the negotiation.

A well-drafted agenda can help you achieve a number of objectives. First, it will force you to organize for the negotiating session and to create priorities. For this reason, an agenda will make the meeting more efficient. Second, the agenda will inform all negotiators about the issues to be discussed at the meeting. This allows proper preparation and can avoid emotional reactions created by surprise. Third, an agenda can be used by a skilled negotiator to create an atmosphere of increasing confidence as each item on the agenda is conquered by the negotiators. Fourth, the agenda can help its creator guide the session toward achieving his or her goals. Fifth, an agenda can create a credible deadline for both parties. If both negotiators recognize a deadline, you can take advantage of the "50 and 10 principle." This negotiating principle holds that 50 percent of the differences between the negotiators will be resolved in the last 10 percent of the negotiation. Finally, the agenda can be used as a standard for judging performance or progress in a negotiation.

Negotiations over the agenda are common. By controlling

the agenda, you can strongly influence the negotiation process. We have repeatedly seen that early success in negotiating the agenda can create momentum for success on more substantive issues. The early success creates an expectation of a positive result that tends to be self-fulfilling. A major part of achieving your desired agreement is simply envisioning the agreement. Because negotiation is a quintessentially human process, it is inevitably fraught with emotional distractions and detours. That is all the more reason for a properly constructed agenda to guide the process.

Three basic questions that should be answered prior to preparing an agenda are: (1) What is the purpose of the meeting? (2) What information will be necessary to make decisions? and (3) Who should attend the meeting? A well-drafted negotiating agenda will:

1. move the process in a positive manner;
2. be well organized but allow others to satisfy their needs within the chosen structure;
3. be informative but not overly detailed;
4. establish priorities;
5. identify the participants; and
6. be circulated in advance.

A good agenda will also indicate, at least by implication, the relative importance of each item. In planning the agenda, carefully consider how and when issues should be introduced. Be sure to give yourself sufficient time to consider proposals. Never accept an agenda proposed by the other negotiator unless you have considered the consequences of accepting the agenda. Study this agenda carefully for what it says about the other party's objectives. Any agenda reveals information on which issues have greatest priority or importance. Be sure to consider what any omissions from the agenda may mean. William Saroyan commented on the informational value of examining omissions when he said: "What people talk about means something. What they don't talk about means something."

Strive to structure the agenda so that the negotiators can work together to generate as many potential ways of reaching an agreement as possible. This brainstorming preferably should begin before the negotiators meet face to face and continue throughout the negotiation. During this brainstorming process, no negotiator should be asked to agree to any specific proposals. "Black and white" thinking should be avoided. If this pre-bargaining brainstorming is effective, a relatively clean and nonjudgmental determination of values, interests, and methods of benefiting the relationship can be achieved. In addition, nothing said during this phase should be used later in the negotiation. All parties should feel free to examine possibilities without implying agreement. This approach has been shown to produce value-creating solutions to seemingly insolvable problems.

The location of negotiations also can favor one side or the other. The agreement of the Western Allies to meet the Soviets in Soviet-controlled Potsdam in 1945 allowed Stalin to manipulate the negotiating environment to his advantage. In a diplomatic setting, therefore, negotiators tend to prefer a neutral setting—such as Malta for the 1989 meeting between Presidents Bush and Gorbachev, Paris for the Vietnam peace talks, Panmunjom for the Korean War talks, or even a raft in the middle of the Neman River when Napoleon Bonaparte and Czar Alexander I met in 1807.

Regardless of the physical location of the negotiation, value-creating solutions are most often found in a nonjudgmental environment. Judging severely inhibits the creative skills that create value in a negotiation. Children are so creative precisely because they have not been taught to be judgmental. If you combine a nonjudgmental attitude with an atmosphere encouraging the exchange of ideas without committing parties to positions, real creativity and value creation are possible.

Be Ready and Rested

He who does not tire, succeeds.

—*Spanish Proverb*

Skilled negotiators avoid situations in which they are not prepared to negotiate. The classic situation where negotiators perform poorly because they are not ready occurs when they receive a telephone call from another negotiator. For some reason, we tend to feel we have an obligation to respond immediately in such a situation. This is a mistake. The person who placed the telephone call probably did so because she felt the timing was right. She probably has all relevant facts and documents supportive of her objectives at hand and may have spoken to experts or advisers just before making the call. Phone calls are also typically made when some event or circumstance has occurred that favors the caller. You, as the recipient of the telephone call, are not likely to have focused on the issue. The relevant documents may not be at hand. You are not ready. In this situation don't start the negotiation. Acknowledge the call and then promise to respond when ready.

A negotiator who has prepared for a meeting and is physically and mentally rested is in the best position to manage the inevitable stress and positively deal with the uncertainty and ever-changing nature of a negotiation. Any negotiator typically will perform worst when the negotiating table is located on another continent. When you are negotiating overseas, your support systems (physical, professional, and emotional) are typically far removed. This obviously can be a considerable disadvantage, heightening the need for thorough preparation before you depart. For example, if you are accustomed to having an accountant run "spread sheets" on a personal computer, you may need to learn how to do it yourself. Arrangements may need to be made for access to a personal computer. Other potential problems need to be anticipated. You may find that a key engineer in the United States is not available when his input is necessary. Because timely access to information and support is crucial to your success in the negotiation, you may need to have key personnel at the home office "standing by" to render any necessary assistance. If necessary, you should travel with or arrange to have access to any people with expertise you may need to call upon during the negotiation.

Being prepared also means being in top mental and physical condition. International negotiation can be physically as well as mentally demanding. The inevitability of travel in international business creates the need to adapt to different cultures, languages, time zones, foods, and lodgings. Beginning serious negotiations without giving yourself sufficient time to overcome jet lag puts you at a distinct disadvantage. Health problems can also drain your stamina. Different food, water, and bacteria can cause all manner of illness, particularly if you do not rest sufficiently after a long trip. It is also wise to avoid too much late-night drinking and entertainment, since jet lag intensifies the usual physical toll on your body. If you find yourself becoming fatigued, adjourn the meeting until you have recovered your strength. Traveling abroad is hard work. The only people who believe that traveling overseas on business is glamorous are people who never travel overseas on business.

Start No Negotiation Before Its Time

Put out your tubs while it is raining.

—Proverb

With someone who holds nothing but trumps, it is impossible to play.

—Friedrich Hebbel

Sometimes, particularly when reading a book like this, you might be led to believe that all problems can be solved by negotiation, provided a constructive and skilled approach is employed. But that's not always the case. Sometimes circumstances do not offer ground for mutual gain. One of the authors was confronted with such a situation while acting on behalf of Flying Tigers, which before its acquisition by Federal Express in 1988 was the world's largest international cargo airline.

Our expert negotiator was sent off on a series of torturous

flights to Malaysia, where the U.S. carrier was having serious problems in its dealing with Malaysian Air System, or MAS, as it is known. The state-owned carrier had been given by its government a monopoly in the ground operations at the Kuala Lumpur airport. All other carriers had no choice but to use MAS for all services they required at that airport. As tends to happen in such circumstances, service levels were poor and price increases were frequent and arbitrary. Our expert negotiator trudged off to this far corner of the planet with a briefcase full of specific problems that needed to be addressed with MAS and detailed solutions to propose for each. This appeared to be an opportune occasion to wield his carefully honed negotiation skills for what certainly must be the mutual benefit of all concerned.

His positive attitude and constructive approach were unscathed when the plenipotentiary of MAS with whom he was scheduled to meet had a minion call Flying Tigers's local office to cancel their appointment, without explanation. This development seemed to fit the modus operandi of the reclusive plenipotentiary. As it was a scant ten minutes before the appointed time, which had been established with great difficulty over a month in advance, our expert felt justified in employing a minor deception. "Tell them I'm already on my way," he sang while dancing out the door. After waiting conspicuously outside the door of the plenipotentiary's office for a couple of hours, ignoring importuning minions, our expert was able at last to gain the audience he sought.

After a few not-so-pleasant pleasantries, our expert cut to the heart of the matter.

"There are a few problems we are having here that we would like to discuss with you," he began.

"There are no problems," the plenipotentiary countered.

"Well, actually," our expert stammered, trying to cut further to the heart of the matter, "I believe you were sent two weeks ago this list of problems and proposed solutions. I brought an extra copy in case yours was misplaced."

"There are no problems," the plenipotentiary repeated heart-lessly.

Our expert suggested that, as we all know, if one party has a problem with a relationship, then there is a problem with the relationship.

"Perhaps rather than discussing the specific problems, we could discuss a general process by which the problems might be reviewed and discussed."

"You don't seem to understand," the plenipotentiary replied, "you have no choice but to procure these services from us. Therefore, as far as we are concerned, there are no problems."

("Doesn't beat around the bush, this one," our expert thought to himself.) "I see," our expert muttered diplomatically, lost in thought. "Let me confirm one thing. Who in your organization is responsible for setting up ground operations in the United States when you begin operations to Los Angeles next year?"

"I am," the plenipotentiary replied smugly.

"Thank you," our expert concluded.

As this story seems to be dragging a bit, we should sum-marize subsequent events. Our expert returned to the United States where he immediately engaged in a dialogue with offi-cials of the U.S. Transportation Department. The subject of this dialogue was the pending application of MAS for authority to serve Los Angeles from Kuala Lumpur. While MAS was entitled to that authority pursuant to a recent aviation agreement be-tween the Malaysian government and the U.S. State Depart-ment, the Transportation Department was empowered to impose conditions on its operating license. Our expert sought a condition that would require that MAS use the aggrieved Flying Tigers for all its ground services in Los Angeles and invoked a law allowing the U.S. government to retaliate against foreign countries who subject U.S. carriers to unfair competitive practices. No such condition had ever been imposed by the United States, and the State Department protested to its brethren at Transportation that such a move would not be well received by the Malaysian government. And, indeed, it wasn't. After several months of passionate and devoted effort, which included hearings before a congressional oversight subcommittee, our expert succeeded in persuading the Transportation Department to include the condition in MAS's U.S. operating license.

Almost a year to the day from our expert's stillborn negotiations in Kuala Lumpur, he was met in his office by a delegation from MAS, led by the esteemed plenipotentiary.

> "Welcome to Los Angeles," our expert gushed, greeting the plenipotentiary. "I really do appreciate your coming all the way across the Pacific to discuss our ground-handling problems in your country."

The negotiations proceeded smoothly, and a solid working relationship was established.

Some negotiations are like negotiating with a defective vending machine. If you put a coin in and nothing comes out, there are a number of things you might do, but one thing is sure: There is no point just talking to it. Developing a sense of when to negotiate and when not to negotiate is important. The skillful use of time is one of the most effective tools of a negotiator. By controlling time, you can control the negotiation process.

There are many times when negotiation is either worthless or counterproductive. It takes at least two to negotiate. Some people pretend to negotiate when their interest is to delay, manipulate, coerce, or sabotage. Often these individuals merely desire to control events to satisfy some personal or institutional inadequacy. Negotiation is also pointless when the best option for the other negotiator is the status quo and you have no ability to impose a sanction. In such a situation, a wise negotiator will not attempt to negotiate.

One key to recognizing when to stop negotiating is noticing when you encounter a pattern of counterproductive behavior from the other negotiator. When unconstructive antics are repeated, odds are that the timing for constructive negotiation is not right. Sometimes only a temporary cessation of negotiations is required. An example of one such situation is where the other negotiators are not listening. People who are angry, for example, are often incapable of listening. Unless the other negotiators are listening, it is not possible to negotiate.

Bear in mind that appearances may indicate a time deadline, while the reality is that you have more time than you think. Deadlines are often artificial constructions to place pressure on the negotiation. Examine any deadline carefully to determine whether it is justified and principled. If you cannot meet a deadline, explain why and inform the other party when you can respond or perform.

Being properly prepared for a negotiation is essential, and you should refuse to begin the negotiations before you are ready. Many bad decisions have been made by negotiators who felt compelled to make a decision on the spot without proper time for preparation and analysis. If you are not prepared to negotiate, your first order of business should be to negotiate for more time.

On the other hand, the process of any negotiation will inevitably present windows of opportunity during which substantial progress is possible. When such a window of opportunity arises, a skilled negotiator will move quickly to seize the day (*carpe diem*). Learning how to identify when the negotiation process has become ripe is best acquired through experience. The best way of describing ripeness may be that moment in time when the negotiators recognize that a proposed exchange of commitments is superior to all alternatives (including the situation as it stands) and maximizes the gain from the exchange.

BARGAINING

Every human benefit and enjoyment, every virtue and every prudent act—is founded upon compromise and barter.

—*Edmund Burke*

The essence of all successful international negotiation is compromise.

—*Sir Anthony Eden*

The terms "bargaining" and "negotiating" are often used as synonyms. It is more accurate to refer to bargaining as only one stage of the negotiation process. Bargaining is the stage in a negotiation when the parties begin working out the division of benefits of the deal. It is during this stage that the value in the transaction is divided by the parties. Negotiation is the entire context in which bargaining occurs. The bargaining stage does not necessarily manifest itself as a discrete time in the overall process, but rather may occur at various levels of intensity throughout the negotiation.

Some bargaining sessions go better than others. A passage from *Aunts Aren't Gentlemen,* by the British humorist P. G. Wodehouse, is illustrative of this point. The dialogue begins when the protagonist in the story spots an item he wishes to purchase from a merchant. He begins the negotiation by asking the price. The merchant responds:

"How much do I want, sir?"

"Yes. Give it a name. We won't haggle."

He pursed his lips. "I'm afraid," he said, having unpursed them, "I couldn't do it as cheap as I'd like, sir . . . I'd have to make it twenty pounds."

I was relieved. I had been expecting something higher. He, too, seemed to feel he had erred on the side of moderation, for he immediately added:

"Or rather thirty."

"Thirty?"

"Thirty, sir."

"Let's haggle," I said.

But when I suggested twenty-five, a nicer looking sort of number than thirty, he shook his grey head regretfully, so we went on haggling, and he haggled better than me, so that eventually we settled on thirty-five.

It wasn't one of my best haggling days.

Build from Small Successes

A journey of a thousand miles must begin with a single step.

—*Lao Tzu*

Little strokes fell great oaks.

—*Benjamin Franklin*

There are three basic approaches to raising issues in a negotiation. Negotiators adopting the first approach begin with the most important and potentially contentious issues. They often do so with the rationale that there is no point to discussing minor issues if major issues cannot be resolved. The second group of negotiators prefers to address smaller and less contentious issues first, saving the more difficult issues for later. This is the approach we favor. The third group of negotiators will address issues in no particular order. While this approach could conceivably be said to offer the advantage of confusing your opposite number as to your objectives and priorities, it more likely reflects just such confusion on your part. In our experience, it is rarely necessary to interject into an international negotiation additional elements of confusion.

Quite often "big" problems can be solved by breaking them down into small, achievable steps. Typically, this will involve getting the other negotiator to say several small yeses rather than one big yes. Small negotiating gains create a climate of success that creates a "winning" atmosphere. The learning process that resulted in the small win can be used to forge agreement on subsequent and progressively more significant issues.

People are naturally attracted to success, particularly when the small wins begin to accumulate. Sports writers are overly apt to refer to this phenomenon as momentum. President Bush, as a candidate, made it famous as the "Big Mo." Whatever its name, momentum is a powerful force once started. Small successes also make the other negotiator feel that he has something invested in the project. Once negotiators have made this emotional investment they are more likely to work to solve problems and are less likely to resist subsequent proposals. As the gains from small successes accumulate, it becomes difficult for the negotiator to return to the situation as it existed before the negotiation began. You are, in effect, creating a constituency that will contribute toward a successful result.

The "small-wins" approach was used effectively by Ambassador Ellsworth Bunker and Panamanian leader Omar Torrijos in the Panama Canal negotiations. Bunker decided to delay discussions on America's rights to indefinitely "defend" the Canal, and Torrijos held off on the question of U. S. payments for use of the Canal. By dealing with lesser issues first, groups that had an interest in advocating a final treaty were established.

Negotiators who do not take the small-wins approach and instead push for the all encompassing "yes" can be successful on occasion but may achieve fewer successes in the long term. People tend to be more comfortable and cooperative when they believe they can achieve a goal and when the personal cost of failure is low. Large problems and concepts can simply overwhelm the other negotiator (not to mention you) because solutions are difficult to conceive. By breaking the process down into smaller parts, its intimidation can be lessened.

In advocating this approach, we should probably interject one caveat. That is, when you are setting the agenda for a given negotiating session, it is probably best not to leave the more difficult or important issues until the very end. Often time constraints will prevent you from completing the agenda, or else the energy and concentration of all involved will have been spent by the time the final agenda items are reached. For this reason, we like to save the final spot on the agenda for those aggravating little issues that may be contentious but ultimately inconsequential. Issues that could lend themselves to endless quibbling when the parties are fresh tend to be dispatched quite readily when the parties are tired and hungry.

Inexperienced negotiators often will try to "cut to the chase" by working immediately to identify differences. This approach is rarely appropriate, as it tends to focus the negotiation on positions rather than interests. Experienced negotiators instead focus first on common ground, the interests the negotiators share. Midway through Henry Kissinger's thirty-five-day shuttle diplomacy that resulted in the 1984 Israeli-Syrian disengagement, a reporter asked Kissinger what he had discussed during those first two weeks. Kissinger responded that he was talking about the principles of a settlement. Some among the press contingent were amazed at this response. The senior correspondent asked incredulously, "How can you talk about principles for two weeks?" One of the other reporters then asked, "Have you got a text?" "No, we don't have a text." "Have you got lines on a map?" "No, we don't have a map." Kissinger knew that it was essential to move the parties toward a common view of a settlement before committing anything to paper. If drafting began before there was a common perception of the objective, arguments over language or lines would doom the negotiation.

International negotiations are likely to require changing or compromising culturally ingrained views or habits (on both sides). For anyone, making changes of a fundamental nature is difficult, to say the least. Organizations like Alcoholics Anonymous have been successful largely because they have recognized that the best way to change behavior is to take small steps. By staying sober for one hour and then for one day, the basic building blocks have been laid. These building blocks can eventually serve as a foundation for the ultimate goal of long-term sobriety.

An example illustrating the small-wins process occurred in Mexico at a manufacturing plant owned by a U.S. multinational company. The products of the plant were plagued by quality problems. A senior manager was sent to Mexico to solve the problem. It took only a few hours for the manager to realize the magnitude of the problems at the plant. Most of the defects were caused by rigid work rules imposed by the union representing the workers. The manager spent two months compiling a list of the necessary changes and then scheduled a meeting with the leaders of the union. The manager could have started his negotiation with the union by asking that all his work rule changes be adopted. This would be a high risk proposition and probably would have been doomed to fail. Instead, the manager chose one small change and asked the union to approve its implementation. The manager promised to give a small merit-salary increase if the change improved quality, provided that the union would agree to adopt a second small change. The union leaders accepted the change because they believed they could convince the membership and saw the cost of failure as being small. When implemented, the change produced significant gains in product quality. Workers and management felt good and were much more receptive to the second change, which was again conditioned upon the acceptance of a third change. The process continued until over 20 changes had been implemented and product quality was approaching 100 percent. The key to the manager's success was making each step appear achievable and minimizing risk. The big gains in quality were produced by many incremental improvements. After a few successes, even one failure can be overlooked and the process of change can continue to a successful conclusion.

Achieving small victories tends to facilitate communication and trust between the negotiators. This trust can be invaluable in resolving more substantial differences. Trust can also expedite the process as the need to independently confirm every statement made by the other negotiator decreases. Albert Einstein's wife was asked if she actually understood the theory of relativity. "No," she answered, "but I know my husband, and I know he can be trusted." So it is in international negotiations. If you know the other negotiator, you can avoid delays caused by mistrust.

You have probably encountered salespeople who have been trained in the "build from small successes" approach to a negotiation. Typically, they will try to get you to agree on less important matters like color or style as they build to the big issue: price and the commitment to buy. After you have answered yes to several questions, it can be hard to say no. This negotiation tactic has been proven to be successful over time by countless salespeople (which may explain that green-checked suit in your closet).

Some people confuse the small-wins approach with a technique known as "salami" negotiating. A former general secretary of Hungary's Communist party described the salami approach as follows:

> When you want to get hold of a salami which your opponents are strenuously defending, you must not grab at it. You must start by carving yourself a very thin slice. The owner of the salami will hardly notice it, or at least he will not mind very much. The next day you will carve another slice, then still another. And so, little by little, the salami will pass into your possession.

The salami technique has a decidedly treacherous sleight of hand feel. It should be distinguished from the small-wins approach, in which the negotiators strive to create momentum and a sense of investment in a relationship through progressively larger incremental gains.

While small successes are the key to big gains, it is important that you have your ultimate sights set on a lofty goal. After you have identified some stratospheric target, then establish lesser, achievable goals that minimize the risk of failure while steadily moving the process ever upward toward the ultimate heights.

Begin by Advancing Your Maximum Credible Position

Ask much, but take as much as they offer.

—*Russian Proverb*

Effectiveness at the conference table depends upon overstating one's demands.

—*Henry Kissinger*

At some point in the negotiating process, one usually struggles with the question of how to set an opening position. At opposite ends of the spectrum are the offer that strains (or exceeds) credibility and the reasonable offer that one expects to be readily accepted. Henry Kissinger is on record as an exponent of the former approach:

> If agreement is usually found between two starting points, there is no point in making moderate offers. Good bargaining technique would suggest a point of departure far more extreme than what one is willing to accept. The more outrageous the initial proposition, the better is the prospect that what one "really" wants will be considered a compromise.

The "reasonable offer" approach is often called Boulwarism, after a now legendary vice president of labor relations at General Electric. In order to avoid the traditional form of bargaining, Mr. Boulware made a careful study of what the employees wanted, and what General Electric could offer, and then presented a best offer to the union's membership on a take-it-or-leave-it basis. Boulware's unorthodox approach and his attempts to bypass the union's leaders by communicating directly with employees were later determined to be an "unfair labor practice" by the National Labor Relations Board. Boulwarism can be just as problematic in international negotiations as it was for old Boulware in his labor negotiations. A British diplomat once said that whenever he encountered a man who claimed to have "all his cards on the table," he was quick to look up each of the man's sleeves.

Neither approach is the preferred alternative in all situations. As a general rule, however, the extreme position is more appropriate the less you know about the situation or the party with whom you are dealing. Negotiating with a total stranger in a foreign culture over an object with which you have no experience or whose value is highly subjective would certainly be a situation that lends itself to a bit of haggling. An extreme position may reveal information about the other party or his or her interest while leaving you room to maneuver. Where you have nearly perfect information, on the other hand, your opening position should approximate your expected outcome. In such a setting, advancing an extreme position would be unproductive game playing. On the New York Stock Exchange, where all traders know the bid and ask prices of a stock and the outcome of its last trade, asking twice the bid price would be a waste of time.

The key here is advancing your maximum **credible** position. An *un*credible position undermines trust and damages the long-term relationship. Where a strong, continuing relationship exists, not only is there a base of information and experience that reduces the need for haggling, but the shared desire to preserve and enhance the relationship moderates the extremity of the parties' positions. Advancing an extreme position with your spouse, for example, is likely only to evidence a lack of consideration and empathy. The value of a strong relationship in facilitating the negotiating process is precisely why we emphasize the importance of building relationships rather than doing deals. A warm and fuzzy relationship can be of great comfort in an often cold and uncertain global business environment.

In addition to its value in revealing information, positional bargaining may be dictated to some extent by cultural variation in the amount of haggling expected in a negotiation. Even among experts, there is often disagreement on how high to set opening positions in a given culture. To paraphrase Rodney Dangerfield, "Take negotiations in Japan. Please." In *Smart Bargaining: Doing Business with the Japanese*, Graham and Sano write:

> In the days of street vendors in Japan banana salesmen were notorious for asking outrageous prices and quickly lowering the prices when faced with buyers' objections. The term **banana no tataki uri** is now used in Japan to describe a similar approach taken by Japanese businesspeople. But instead of bananas, factories, distribution chains, even banks are sometimes bargained for using the "banana sale" approach. Japanese executives are more likely to use such a tactic during international negotiations because they don't know what to expect from foreign buyers and they feel that it's safer to leave room to maneuver.

In a chapter in the book *National Negotiating Styles*, Thayer and Weiss disagree:

The Japanese do not deliberate extensively over their bargaining tactics or plan what concessions they might make. . . . when the Japanese do present a first proposal, it is carefully drafted and reasonable. It reflects the Japanese predilection for well-informed, "best" solutions and the solidarity (and obligation) arising from domestic consensus-building.

To be fair, Graham and Sano were concentrating on business-men and Thayer and Weiss on government officials. But the differences between these two opinions on the appropriate opening position when negotiating with Japanese are too strik-ing to be explained away by this one variable.

The experience of an American company reporting the taxes of its subsidiary in Italy is illustrative of culturally mandated haggling. The Italian tax system on its face is similar to the system that exists in the United States. However, the common practice is for Italian corporations to submit a return that sub-stantially understates profits. An Italian company may typically understate its profits by anywhere from 30 percent to 80 per-cent. The tax authorities in Italy are operating under this as-sumption and approximately six months after a return is filed may issue an "invitation to discuss" the tax return. During this discussion, the Italian tax authorities will make a tax assessment that is based on a multiple of the amount of actual profits reported. Intentional understatement matched by intentional overstatement then forms the basis for subsequent negotia-tions. These negotiations are so culturally entrenched that a specialized professional known as a "commercialista" typically will be engaged to negotiate with the Italian tax officials. The commercialista will charge a lump-sum fee for his services. Reportedly, a portion of this fee has been known to find its way to the Italian tax authorities. This payment is what Italians call "bustarella."

The American company involved in this example was advised to file an Italian-style income tax return, understating income and, therefore, substantially underestimating the taxes due. The American manager rejected this advice and instead filed an American-style tax return which fairly and accurately re-flected the company's obligations under the law. Approximately six months later, the American company received an "invitation to discuss" the tax return from the Italian tax authorities. Instead of hiring a commercialista, the American manager wrote a letter to the Italian tax authorities stating that his company's return was accurate and requesting clarification on the specific items that were in question. The manager received no response to the particulars of his letter, but instead received a formal assessment that imposed a tax that was 600 percent of the amount stated in the company's American-style return. The American manager was agitated, to say the least, and arranged to meet personally with the Italian tax authorities. At the meeting, the American manager expressed his disbelief that such an assessment could be imposed. He argued vigorously that there was absolutely no justification for the higher assessment. The Italian tax official responded: "You may be right, but now we have your attention. Shall we begin the negotiations?" The subsequent negotiations went poorly and the American company ended up paying twice the taxes it reported in its American-style tax return. A few months later the American manager was managing a manufacturing plant in Des Moines, Iowa.

Another, perhaps obvious, advantage of starting with an extreme position is that the other party just may accept it. On several occasions, we've advanced positions that were only barely compatible with a straight face, only to have them accepted with little or no modification. It makes you wonder if you were a chump on all those occasions you advanced a "reasonable" position. It's safe to say that you probably won't get something if you don't ask for it.

An investment banker from New Zealand tells the following story about the negotiation of a fee with a client:

My immediate superior in the bank was a Mr. T who had the gift of the Irish and was never short of a good story.

We had been mandated to complete an intricate on-shore/offshore tax-driven financing for a major corporate client. The transaction would give an enhanced bottom line to the company yet was marginal when one considered the risk of the Tax Commissioner's intervention. As such, each party had their lawyers present when the transaction details were in part revealed to the company directors. We could not disclose the offshore "black box" where the benefits to the corporate client arose. However, as this was our role, this was what we were being paid for.

I had imagined we would be looking for a fee based on the usual factors, that is, size, risk, additional expertise, etcetera, so had in mind a fee of around $100,000. To my surprise, Mr. T nonchalantly dropped into the conversation that the fee would be $250,000. The room went silent. As a novice to this side of the table, I felt embarrassed. Not to be placed off his stride, Mr. T continued, still smiling while clarifying to our client that he meant a "net-fee" of $250,000.

"What do you mean by that?" asked the Managing Director.

"Well, it works like this, you pay us the $250,000 and you pay all legal bills including those that come in from New York, the Bahamas, Hong Kong and of course your own New Zealand lawyers and ours." Mr. T sailed on, "Now we can't guarantee how much these will be, after all a New York lawyer charges like a wounded bull and they don't take into account the exchange rate to New Zealand dollars or anything else so this could be any amount. There can't be any guarantee at all—I mean the accounts could be coming in for months."

Our lawyer said nothing and I assumed he agreed with all that had been said. Mr. T had by now picked up on the agitation of our client, who was just discovering the actual costs of such a transaction.

Capitalizing on the moment, and working on the assumption that two negatives can make a positive, he diverted attention away from the $250,000 and moved on:

"I can understand your position being faced with the uncertainty of the overseas lawyers. After all *we* all know how much this can amount to. . . ."

Everyone nodded, while really having no idea at all.

". . . tell you what I'll do for you. Increase our fee to $350,000 and we'll meet *all* legal bills and disbursements. I am sorry but that really is the best I can do even if it means we get less out of the deal. We're here for your benefit after all."

The directors, with the burden of ongoing liabilities lifted from their shoulders, thought that Mr. T's suggestion was terrific.

Our lawyer said nothing. It was only as we went back to our office that Mr. T told me he had only ever used a New York lawyer once for something totally different. As it turned out, our total legal bills and disbursements amounted to less than $40,000.

I had learned my first lesson in negotiations: "If the music is too loud, turn it up."

Many studies have been conducted to determine how a person's level of aspiration relates to the result achieved in a negotiation. In one study, the negotiators were informed that they could participate in a second, more profitable negotiation if their agreed price exceeded $2.00. A second group of negotiators was told that they could move to the more profitable negotiation with an agreed price above $6.00. Both groups received an identical fact situation. The statistical average for the first group was approximately $2.43 and for the second $6.25. Other research conducted by Rubin and Brown has established that "bargainers attain higher and more satisfactory outcomes when they begin their interaction with extreme rather than moderate demands." This is another way of saying that negotiators who expect more from a negotiation tend to get more.

Most experienced negotiators prefer to have the other party make the first offer in a negotiation. The party who moves first gives away information without the benefit of another offer as a reference point. Few people knew the value of making the second responsive effort in a negotiation better than the legendary studio founder Samuel Goldwyn. Goldwyn always liked to gain the upper hand in a negotiation. On one occasion, Goldwyn wanted to borrow an actor from Darryl Zanuck. Goldwyn had been trying to speak with Zanuck for several hours but was told the studio head was in an important conference. Zanuck's secretary finally put Goldwyn through after she became convinced of the urgency of the call. When Zanuck an-

swered the telephone, Goldwyn began the conversation by saying: "Darryl! What can I do for you today?"

A friend of ours recounts an experience in Indonesia. He
desired a gold claim owned by an ethnic Chinese merchant,
and this became known in the social stratosphere of Jakarta.
By chance, our friend and the Chinese merchant were invited
to the same dinner party. After dinner, our friend approached
the owner of the coveted claim.

"Good to see you," said our friend.

"Likewise," responded the Chinese merchant.

"I suppose you've heard I would like to buy your gold claim,"
our friend said, somewhat hesitantly.

The Chinese merchant said nothing and his face was expres-
sionless. The silence became awkward for our friend, so he continued,

"So, how much are you asking?"

The Chinese merchant chuckled and said, "It is not I who
wishes to sell. It is you who wishes to buy."

Our friend was forced to make the first offer on the gold claim.

In some industries, whoever makes the first offer is determined by convention. In real estate, for example, the seller, in
listing the property, makes the first offer. Situations may be
encountered, however, in which neither party is willing to
make the first offer. One way of resolving such a positional-
bargaining impasse is to ask both parties to exchange a summary of the interests they wish to advance, without including
specific means of achieving those interests. The goal of this
exercise is to provide both parties with information on the other's interests that can be used to create options in lieu of positions. This process of creating, refining, and selecting among
options may be carried out all the way to agreement without
either side having to adopt a position.

When the time comes to begin transferring value, you should

have determined in advance which negotiating points have the smallest cost to you and the greatest value to the other negotiator. More than **what** you give up is important. **How** you transfer value can be equally important. Begin transferring value slowly and in small increments. Always strive to obtain value for the value you give. Transferring value in progressively smaller increments to indicate you are approaching a limit can be a useful technique. Try to think through the principles that support your position and militate against its being altered further. You should think through principles and positions together.

Then there's the "fallacy of precision," which can work for or against you. Greater precision in a figure implies precision in the method of its determination. Economists are particularly inclined to generate precise forecasts based on imprecise assumptions. On the other hand, a round figure can serve as a starting point or as a compromise without attracting attention to the details underlying it. Similarly, a principle may be found simply in splitting the difference.

The ancient and time-tested "let's split it 50-50" approach was given an odd twist in an incident recounted by Ambassador Edward L. Rowny. The negotiation occurred during a U.S.-Soviet boat ride on Lake Geneva:

> I began playing my harmonica in an effort to encourage friendlier interactions with the Soviets. Our secretaries danced with the Soviets, and everyone had a good time. At the end of the festivities, the head of the Soviet SALT I delegation, Vladimir Semenov, took up a collection of rubles, dollars, and French and Swiss francs. He grinned and said "O.K., we will split it 50-50." Then he put all the money in his pocket. "What do you mean 50-50," I asked. And he replied, "Well, you had 50 percent of the pleasure by playing. I get 50 percent of the pleasure by spending the money."

The Soviet's ploy is a variation of the "heads I win, tails you lose" technique.

Making that last concession can be as problematic as setting the opening position. In one important international negotiation, the principals started out $20 million apart. The American wanted $80 million for his financial services business. The Hong Kong Chinese executive offered $60 million. Over time, the Hong Kong executive raised his bid to $75 million, and the American dropped his asking price to $76.3 million. In the final meeting, the $1.3 million difference remained unchanged for hours, with the American seemingly ready to walk away from the deal that offered over $20 million in profit to him. Eventually, the Hong Kong executive raised his offer to $76 million. But when he asked the American to drop his demand for the last $300,000, the American's answer was, "No way, $76.3 million is my final offer."

As a final gesture to overcome the impasse, the American suggested they flip a coin for the difference. The Hong Kong executive looked around the room at his colleagues in disbelief. "Flip for it?" he asked. "For $300,000?" Moments later, the Hong Kong executive tossed a quarter into the air. The American's call of "tails" was answered with the stern profile of George Washington. He had just increased his fortune by millions—but not by the last $300,000.

Maintain Leverage by Creating and Preserving Alternatives

Necessity never made a good bargain.

—Benjamin Franklin

When a prince or a state is powerful enough to dictate to his neighbors, the art of negotiation loses its value.

—François de Callières

During the negotiation process decisions about whether to accept a given offer must be analyzed against a base point. This base point is what Fisher and Ury refer to as your Best Alternative To a Negotiated Agreement (BATNA). Your BATNA sets the base point that any negotiated structure must exceed if agreement is to be reached. It is important not to get swept away in the momentum of a negotiation without making the basic evaluation of a proposed agreement: Is it better than the alternative? Of course, if you are to make that evaluation, you must have first thought through or investigated your alternatives to the deal being negotiated. This formulation of alternatives should be an active progress—go about creating alternatives. Viewing the negotiating progress from a dynamic, relationship-building viewpoint rather than from a static, deal orientation, should lead one to preserve alternatives as well as create them. Moreover, a better result is usually obtained if those you are negotiating with are aware that you have attractive alternatives to concluding a deal with them. It keeps them on their toes. If they have done their homework, it may not even be necessary to enlighten them on this point yourself. The grapevine in foreign countries can amaze even the most grizzled veteran of international negotiations.

Which leads us to what seems to be a basic law of negotiation: negotiators who are not dependent on the object of the negotiation will tend to achieve a better result. Imagine negotiating with an antique dealer over the price of an object you really do not want that badly. You will probably be able to obtain a better price because of your indifference. Conversely, an item you simply can't do without will nearly always come at a dear price. A trip to this same antique dealer may reveal another phenomenon. Many of us have made what we feel is a low-ball offer only to have it readily accepted. The feeling one gets in this situation is an example of what has been called "the winner's curse." Human nature causes us to question whether we have been cheated when our offer is accepted too quickly. Some academic observers believe that this winner's curse results from one side clearly having better information. The merchant deals in the item every day and knows the market price. The buyer typically does not have the same advantage. The key to avoiding the winner's curse and to obtaining the best possible negotiated result is seeking out information that will put you in a stronger informational position relative to the merchant than you otherwise would be. This means researching the market and seeking information from the merchant through listening and careful observation. This information should be obtained before you make an offer. If you do not have good information, it is better to start with an extreme bid. As you moderate your position, you should be acquiring information on the market price of the item through dialogue. You may even discover that your extreme position wasn't that far off the mark.

Maintaining leverage by preserving alternatives helps not only in achieving the best bargain, but also in securing the benefits of that bargain over time. Americans' noble political tradition tends to lead them to think of their "rights" in any given situation. They expect disputes to be resolved by reference to some external independent standard. Laws, regulations, the common law, contracts, or social custom can all in proper circumstances create a belief in negotiators that they have certain "rights." But rights in an international negotiation are usually unclear and often conflict depending upon which standard is used as a reference. This tendency to think in terms of rights is not easily abandoned when Americans become involved in international transactions. While remaining philosophically neutral on the subject of natural rights, we recommend a more practical approach to international dealings. Rather than considering yourself to have "rights," view yourself as having "interests" that must be protected. The former foreign minister of France, Maurice-Jacques Couve de Murville, has said: "One does not negotiate in order to conclude something, but to ensure the triumph of the interests in one's charge."

The experience of a senior American negotiator for a large U.S. industrial company illustrates the problems that can result from undue reliance on contracts. The American company entered into a technology license agreement with a mid-size Korean company. After a relatively smooth start, a dispute developed with respect to the licensor's obligation to provide technical assistance and the costs to be borne by the licensee. The licensor's representatives came to Korea to address the problems and found themselves in a meeting with the president of the Korean company and half a dozen minions.

The Americans were surprised to hear their Korean counterparts raise exactly the same issues that were discussed in the original negotiation. Each time the Korean side raised an issue, the Americans pointed to the appropriate clause and smugly asserted that the matter had been agreed to, codified in the agreement, executed by the Korean president and approved by the Ministry of Trade and Industry. After several repetitions of this scenario, the Korean president said, "Let me see that agreement." After it was handed to him, the Americans watched in amazement as he ripped it up and dropped the pieces into a trash can. He returned to the negotiating table, smiled and said, "Now we can proceed to address the matters at hand."

The American parties at first took this as evidence that the Koreans were crooks who had no qualms about going back on their word at the least provocation. Exercising a degree of patience, they listened to the specific problems outlined by the Korean side. While it was true that the Koreans had been overly optimistic about their ability to absorb the technology, commence production, and pay royalties, the parties were able to hammer out a compromise under which the relationship survived, albeit with some concessions on the part of the licensor.

The American negotiator later told us: "I learned three important lessons in negotiating with Koreans. First, Koreans look at a signed agreement as a starting point, not a final expression of the future course of events. 'How can an agreement predict the future?' the President had said. Second, Koreans believe in fate, not fault. They did not understand that they would be expected to bear the burden created by their own miscalculations. Any change in the situation is viewed as an act of God. Thus, the other party should share the burden and have been willing to compromise, even after obtaining firm commitments in the signed agreement. And third, they may have planned it this way from the beginning. More caution should be exercised in the original negotiation. The fact that Koreans may ignore specific terms of the agreement makes the agreement more important, not less. Careful negotiation and drafting may create incentives that will avoid the type of hedging encountered here. Advance payments, penalties, offsets, and the like which are outside their control will prevent them from whipsawing the foreign party."

Americans are accustomed to relying on contracts and a familiar and relatively equitable legal system. Contracts are rarely easier to enforce in foreign countries than in the United States, and achieving a remedy based on the legal merits involved in a case may be impossible. This is not intended to suggest the inferiority of any particular legal system (our own certainly falls somewhat short of perfection). Rather, it is inherent in the geographic and cultural distances involved.

Of course, it is possible to encounter less efficient legal systems than our own. An experienced lawyer once described a lawsuit in India as the nearest thing to eternal life ever seen on the face of this earth. The chief justice of India has publicly stated that the Indian judicial system is on the verge of collapse. At the time of the chief justice's comments, well over one million cases were on appeal. One must bear such legal efficiencies in mind when involved in international negotiation.

Bringing a lawsuit or submitting a matter to arbitration to resolve a dispute is nearly always a last resort when doing business with a foreign company. Lawyers' fees and costs associated with transnational litigation or arbitration can escalate at a rate that makes an adversarial resolution to an international dispute cost-effective only if huge amounts are at stake. Litigation, particularly international litigation, is expensive. Since attorneys' fees are often not recoverable even if you are successful, any amount received from a court judgment or arbitral award may only be sufficient to pay your lawyer. The time lost and brain damage sustained in the process are gone forever.

Rather than relying on contracts, lawyers, and courts to protect your interests when dealing internationally, you are better off maintaining some form of continuing leverage. Continuing leverage just means that you are able to hold out some incentive for the other side to continue honoring the agreement. The greater the benefits to be derived from an agreement, the greater the incentive to comply with its terms. The incentive to comply with an agreement can also be created if costs will be incurred by the foreign party in the event of noncompliance. Again, the greater the potential cost or benefit, the greater the incentive to comply with an agreement.

American diplomats negotiating with the Soviets over housing for diplomatic staff failed to provide for continuing leverage and paid the price. An agreement was reached with the Soviets allowing their diplomats to occupy an apartment complex they had constructed in Washington, D.C., in return for which apartments would be found for U.S. diplomats in Moscow. Once the Soviets moved into their apartments, however, the U.S. leverage was gone. The Soviets had little incentive to provide satisfactory apartments for the Americans unless concessions were offered in some other area. Even then, the Americans were chided for wanting to link "apples with oranges."

Leverage at the time a deal is concluded is not enough. The leverage must continue until the benefit of the bargain has been realized if it is to be fully effective. There are various types of incentives that create continuing leverage. Some examples include future improvements in technology, funds not released under a letter of credit, additional business in the future, continued access to a crucial component or raw material, access to additional capital, skilled workers or managers, and access to existing distribution networks.

When people evaluate the outcome of a negotiation, you will often hear the more cynical observers recite the so-called golden rule of business—He who has the gold, makes the rules. It is generally true that the more powerful negotiator will receive the lion's share of the benefits in a negotiation. But what is less clear is what creates "power" in a negotiation. Power is the ability directly or indirectly to influence the outcome of the negotiation, which usually means the decisions or behavior of the other party.

In assessing how power influences a negotiation, consider the following:

1. Power in a negotiation is created by the perceptions of the negotiators about their ability to influence each other. The factors that create power are need, desire, and alternatives. The relative influence of these factors is usually changing constantly over time. Factors that could influence another negotiator but that are not perceived by a negotiator are irrelevant (at least until they are perceived). If the other party perceives that you can influence him or her, you have power.

2. Power is not necessary to create an incentive to negotiate. It is enough for a successful negotiation if an exchange of

commitments can remedy or improve the position of each negotiator.

3. Because power is a perceived ability to influence the other negotiator, do not assume that the other negotiator knows your weaknesses. Wait until you have objective evidence that the other negotiator recognizes your inability to influence him or her before relinquishing power.

4. Power may be exercised without mention or use. Power may also be diminished by its exercise or threatened exercise. Negative incentives or sanctions, for example, can severely damage a relationship. The degree of one's power is measured by the ability to achieve a given result with the least effort or expenditure.

Of course, there is a difference between real power and perceived power. We have all been in positions where our real power is weak but our perceived power is enough to achieve an objective. A client of ours who has purchased men's apparel in India for over a decade tells the story of the time he was able to negotiate his best price ever for men's shirts with a manufacturer at a time when he desperately needed the shirts to fill an order that had been damaged during shipment. The Indian manufacturer thought it was "after the season" and thus considered himself lucky he could sell any shirts at all. The Indian manufacturer falsely perceived he had no power because he had incomplete information.

Be Patient

He that can have patience can have what he will.

—*Benjamin Franklin*

All human error is impatience, a premature renunciation of method, a delusive pinning down of a delusion.

—*Franz Kafka*

The communication between human beings can be divided into four categories based upon purpose. These categories are:

1. **Phatic:** This type of communication consists of the preliminary discussions that are intended to build a binding personal relationship. Phatic communication is particularly important because we communicate at a higher level with people with whom we have created a personal bond.

2. **Informational:** The sharing of information is the second and most obvious purpose of communication. This type of communication allows individuals to share ideas with others. How well a person is about to transmit, receive, interpret, and respond to others will determine his or her effectiveness at communicating on this level.

3. **Persuasive:** This third type of communication takes place when one person desires to persuade another. A communicator seeking to persuade another person will be most effective if he or she is a willing and able listener. Affecting a person's behavior and reinforcing or instilling beliefs in another person can be accomplished best if that person is conscious of the message. In some cases, however, the same result can be achieved even though the person is not conscious that he or she has been persuaded.

4. **Cathartic:** The purpose of this type of communication is the release of emotions. The need to share emotions with another person relates to both positive and negative emotions. For this form of communication to be effective, the listener must be willing and able to accept the conduct of the person seeking a cathartic release.

The phatic aspect of communication tends to be the most neglected by Americans in their international dealings. When two individuals are engaged in phatic communication, information is being exchanged that is not directly relevant to the substance of the negotiation. To those more concerned with effecting than dissecting communication, this is called "small talk." (Dogs refer to this as the "sniffing stage.") While Americans are generally accustomed to this part of the negotiation process, we may consider a ten-minute exchange of pleasantries perfectly appropriate before "getting down to business." In most other cultures a significantly longer period is required before beginning discussions on substantive matters.

One of the authors was present at an initial session between an American and an Indonesian company during which nothing other than golf was discussed. The Japanese often conduct *aisatsu*, which refers to the initial meeting held by two high-level executives from different companies. This meeting begins the relationship between the parties. Business is not discussed since the sole purpose is to exchange greetings. Negotiations begin at a later time.

The best explanation we've heard of the value of small talk came from a wizened Brazilian businessman. When we asked him why negotiations moved so slowly in the early stages in South America, he answered poetically:

"We don't negotiate with strangers. Until we know the person, it is pointless to discuss matters of substance."

We have found this principle to be invaluable whatever the setting of the negotiations. By working to turn a stranger into someone you know, you create a relationship.

The small talk phase is perhaps the most important part of the negotiating process in an international context. The stages that follow are unlikely to be successful if this earlier stage is a failure. For this reason, the informal conversation and social events that occur throughout an international negotiation can be crucial. We know of more than one American negotiating team that became so perplexed by their failure to make progress in a negotiation that they declined all evening social invitations from their foreign counterparts so they could solicit instructions from headquarters and evaluate the day's activities among themselves. What these American negotiators apparently did not realize is that the negotiations will not be allowed to progress until the foreign negotiators are able to understand their counterparts as people. As a rule, the more consequential and long term the deal under discussion, the more time and effort will need to be spent developing a relationship before beginning substantive discussions.

This particularly American desire for expeditious entry into the heart of the matter was exhibited by Franklin Roosevelt at the end of World War II at the famous Yalta conference. Before the meeting, Roosevelt and Churchill met to discuss strategy. Roosevelt expressed his hope that the meetings with Stalin would not last more than five or six days. Churchill replied: "I do not see any way of realizing our hopes about world organization in five or six days. Even the Almighty took seven." The extent to which American expectations of the duration of a negotiation can differ from those of a foreign foe was demonstrated yet again when peace talks to end the Vietnam War began in Paris. The American negotiators, led by Averell Harriman, checked into the Ritz Hotel, while the North Vietnamese leased a villa for two years.

Among those with a deal orientation rather than a relationship orientation, the preliminary discussions that do not concern business, or the informal socializing that inevitably accompanies international negotiations, may be viewed as a waste of time. They are not. Turning a stranger into a friend (or at least a known adversary) cannot be accomplished in an instant. Developing the relationships that are necessary to deal across a dozen time zones can take time and a lot of effort.

While being patient is important, you must be "aggressively persistent" in seeking what you desire. Miyamoto Musashi, the Japanese military strategist, wrote on this approach:

> Both in fighting and in everyday life you should be determined though calm. Meet the situation without tenseness yet not recklessly, your spirit settled yet unbiased.

Simply waiting for a desired result is not sufficient. You must be actively pressing for movement and yet patient for the result. In this process, subtle judgment is required. It is a matter of learning to swim strongly when the tide is with you and resting when the tide is reversed.

A cross-cultural negotiation will nearly always require more time to complete than a negotiation between compatriots. The extra time is entailed, in part, in observing the proper protocol and developing the necessary relationship between the parties.

As with much in life, how the result is obtained can be as important as the result itself.

Being patient for gain from a negotiation shouldn't be confused with foregoing gain from the negotiation. The People's Republic of China has been effective in negotiations with foreign firms by dangling the carrot of access to the world's most populous market. This lure has been caricatured in the premise, "If everyone bought only one shoe." The PRC is now littered with corpses of foreign firms who went into deals in the 1970s and 1980s dreaming of future riches. There is much truth to the saying that "The PRC is the country of the future . . . and always will be."

Give Face

The most advantageous negotiations are those one conducts with human vanity, for one obtains very substantial things from it while giving very little of substance in return. One never does so well when dealing with ambition or avarice.

—Alexis de Tocqueville

The concept of "face" is often misunderstood. Face is an outward concept—the opposite of shame; it should be distinguished from guilt or pride, which are inward concepts. While many people associate face only with Asian cultures, it can be an important concept in all cultures. Less well known than the concept of losing face is "giving" face. This occurs when you contribute to the outward respect or prestige of the other party. Flattery, in contrast, appeals to one's inner vanities. Both may engender goodwill toward you, and both are important. Giving face, however, may contribute positively to the effectiveness of your counterpart, thereby increasing the value he can contribute to the relationship.

Fundamentally, you give face when you allow the other negotiator to achieve a result that is consistent with his or her principles or previous statements and actions. It is pretty basic that making a person look good can have enormous importance in a negotiation, while causing damage to the standing of one's counterpart can have severe adverse effects. These things can be subtle, though. For example, when negotiating with foreigners, an American may naturally begin talking to the member of the foreign negotiating team who has the best English-language skills. In so doing, however, one may be undercutting the authority of a senior negotiator, thereby causing loss of face. By associating yourself with a lower-level player on the other side you may also be lowering your own status. This is another example of the subtle dangers of ethnocentrism. The person who speaks the best English is not necessarily the most important (or most intelligent) person on the other negotiating team.

United States Treasury Department Undersecretary for International Affairs in the Bush administration, David Mulford, could have benefited from a few lessons in giving face in his negotiations over the restructuring of Mexico's foreign debt. The *Wall Street Journal* recounted this incident in a front-page story:

> One evening [in July 1989] after months of talks with U.S. bankers, the top members of Mexico's negotiating team began collecting their papers from a conference room in the Treasury Building. Suddenly, Mr. Mulford strode into the room. He glanced around and turned to Pedro Aspe, the finance minister of Mexico. "What have you got your [expletive] numbers guys here for?" he demanded. Mr. Mulford later said he was frustrated because the Mexican staffers were making it impossible to reach a deal. But the Mexicans never forgot the insult and some, mocking the undersecretary, still jokingly refer to each other as "[expletive] numbers guys."

There are usually much more subtle ways of accomplishing an objective than causing a person to lose face in front of others. If criticism becomes necessary, do it in private. Try to buffer the criticism by mixing in some positive observations. One does not need to be direct in criticizing a subordinate. For example, in Taiwan an American manager, fluent in Chinese, who spots an incorrect Chinese character in a report could call in the subordinate and indicate the mistake. This creates friction because the foreigner has made a direct criticism as well as strayed from his role as a foreigner. If the American manager instead calls in the subordinate and states that he did not know the Chinese character could be used in that way, the error is spotted and direct confrontation is avoided. In cultures where intermediaries play a key role in nurturing relationships, it may be useful to convey criticism through this person, particularly if the other party involved is of high social status. Bad feelings, once created, can be difficult or impossible to eliminate. If ill feelings do exist, it is often useful to involve a mediator who can assist you in repairing the damaged relationship.

Foreign negotiators, like all of us, need to justify their existence. They need to feel they have contributed to the effort. By structuring an initial offer so as to leave room to grant more favorable terms during the negotiation, you will often be in a position to allow the foreigner to feel good about his or her role in the negotiation. By obtaining "concessions" from you during the negotiation, the foreign negotiator can return to face his or her colleagues with pride and a sense of accomplishment. We have repeatedly found that a proposed agreement is more likely to be accepted if it allows all parties involved in the negotiation process to justify their existence by contributing to the result in some way. The sometimes protracted process during which negotiators move toward agreement through offer and counteroffer may be frustrating, but it is useful. The process may be formalistic in nature, but it is nearly always meeting a need of one or the other negotiator. Both sides are able to garner a sense of self-importance and to create an atmosphere of progress. This momentum will often carry over to the relationship and can assist in creating a successful venture.

In addition to giving face, it is important to accept your counterparts as they are. In so doing, you help avert disputes arising from differences between personalities rather than differences concerning issues or interests. Arguments and disputes can be avoided by focusing on **what** is right, rather than **who** is right. Work to keep your focus on resolving substantive **problems** and not on your differences with **people.**

Explain Rather Than Argue or Coerce

Would you seek to persuade, speak of interest not of reason.

—Benjamin Franklin

I never saw an instance of one or two disputants convincing the other by argument. I have seen many, on getting warm, becoming rude and shooting one another.

—Thomas Jefferson

Perhaps the most effective strategy for achieving success in any negotiation is being able to present your proposals so that your counterparts see your position as a previously unrealized objective. This typically entails changing the other negotiator's perspective on the issue under consideration. Convincing by logic is less important than finding a position that satisfies the needs, interests, and expectations of each negotiator. Your goal is to create a solution that is acceptable from two different perspectives by reconciling interests. The opposite and least effective negotiating technique is trying to convince your foreign counterpart to "change his mind" through the strength or logic of your arguments. It is difficult to change interests by arguing. Oliver Wendell Holmes once said: "Deep-seated preferences cannot be argued about—you cannot argue a man into liking a glass of beer." While ends are seldom arguable, means are.

Persuasion is commonly thought to be the result of verbal arguments. "I talked her into it" can be heard from many a boastful persuader. Often, however, nonverbal means can be used to produce the desired response. A well-timed pause, smile, polite gesture, or look of interest or concern can be more persuasive than a long-winded, self-important lecture on the merits of your position. When you argue, your opinion is placed in opposition to that of your counterpart. If you force him to withdraw his opinion, you have won and he has lost. You have won the battle but may doom yourself to losing the war. Arguments produce plenty of heat but little warmth.

We have learned over time that listening "wins" more arguments than arguing. Most people will form the highest opinion of you if you let them do all the talking. We often hear second-hand about a great conversation we had with some person, when we did little or no talking. Listening also uncovers new information that can be used in crafting solutions that create gain through reconciling interests.

Arguments are also dangerous in that it is easy to lose your temper in the face of a dispute. Once you let negative emotions creep into an argument, the negative emotion is itself a rebuttal of your position. The best way to avoid arguments is to avoid expressing opinions. Benjamin Franklin made this point well when he said in his autobiography:

> I made it a rule to forebear all direct contradiction to the sentiments of others, and all positive assertion of my own. I even forbid myself . . . the use of every word or expression in the language that imported a fix'd opinion, such as certainly, undoubtedly, etc., and I adopted, instead of them, I conceive, I apprehend, or I imagine a thing to be so or so; or it so appears to me at present.

It is generally more productive to explain the benefits of your proposal in a manner that reveals it to be an objective the other side never recognized rather than presenting arguments or logic supporting your position. In explaining why a particular action is favorable to your counterpart, there is seldom a situation where a didactic or paternalistic approach will be most effective. In fact, the more subtle and less direct your explanation, the more likely you are to succeed. People are more likely to be convinced by reasons they discovered themselves than by reasons pointed out to them by others. The most skillful form of persuasion often is to guide the other person through questions or observations to his own "original" conclusion or insight. This idea was well articulated by the British philosopher, professor, and humorist C. Northcote Parkinson in the context of a grant application:

> It is the essence of grantsmanship to persuade the Foundation executives that it was *they* who suggested the research project

and that you were a belated convert, agreeing reluctantly to what they had proposed.

While it is possible to guide a person in this manner to a change of mind, it is nearly impossible to bring another person to acknowledge that you have caused him to change his mind. Nobody likes to "eat crow" or lose face. Strive to avoid putting the other person in the position of admitting, even to himself, that his mind has been changed.

Preempt Problems

A verbal contract is not worth the paper it's written on.

—Samuel Goldwyn

Americans' deal orientation leads us to put stock in the precise terms of a written agreement. Someone from a more relationship-oriented culture is more likely to construe contractual obligations loosely, as subject to revision if the needs or objectives of one side change in a material way. The American should not conclude from this, however, that the precise terms of the agreement are unimportant. The process of negotiating a contract allows the parties to ensure that they have a shared view of their responsibilities in the relationship. For this reason, it is wise to document the agreement in simple, understandable terms so that the responsibilities and rights of both sides are clear. No one feels obligated to honor a provision they never understood. Even if you have the ability to force compliance with a contractual provision your counterpart never fully understood before signing an agreement, the relationship may be severely damaged in the long run.

While it may be tempting to do so, you should not ignore difficult issues with the hope that the issue may never arise or the fear that working through the problem will spoil the relationship. Without mutual understanding and a full meeting of the minds, the necessary relationship may be fatally flawed. The difficult issues are hidden mines that could explode at the least opportune time. In any negotiation it is important that you determine the motives and objectives of your counterpart and determine whether they are compatible with your own. This process is of heightened importance in international negotiations because of the differences in values, ethics, etiquette, customs, and beliefs that motivate the two sides. The other side may have motives and objectives entirely different from what you think, with misunderstanding and miscalculation the result.

The importance of clarifying objectives at the outset of the relationship was illustrated by a rather typical joint venture between an American semiconductor manufacturer and a Korean conglomerate with the production of semiconductors as its purpose. The objective of the American manufacturer was fairly straightforward by American standards: earn the highest return possible on the investment and pay dividends to the U.S. parent company with these earnings so that the price of the parent company's stock will rise. The American company assumed that the objectives of the Korean company were the same. After all, what could be more important than maximizing the return on investments and increasing the price of your stock? In this example, the Korean conglomerate was owned by one family and had a high level of debt relative to equity. Financial reporting practices in Korea are poor (as they are in much of the developing world), so the loans that made up the Korean conglomerate's debt were given by banks more on the basis of reputation than earnings. Thus, the Korean conglomerate's objective was to increase sales and market share, even if return on investment was lowered. The Korean conglomerate was also being pressured by its government to hire more employees to reduce the nation's high unemployment rate. Additional government pressure was placed on the Korean conglomerate not to declare dividends from the joint venture since the American company would remit profits to its parent company in United States dollars, and thus reduce Korea's foreign exchange reserves. Given the differing objectives of the American company and the Korean conglomerate, it is not surprising that major disputes arose over business strategy and dividend policy, none of which had been addressed in the parties' joint-venture agreement.

If the objectives of the parties appear to be inconsistent, it is all the more important that their reconciliation be spelled out in a clear agreement. In the above situation, the American company should have sought a contractual method of determining when dividends would be paid—for example, if profits were above a certain level. Resolving the differing objectives concerning profits versus market share and turnover is more problematic. Perhaps these objectives could not have been reconciled. But if that was the case, then the parties needed to know that when they were negotiating the terms of the joint-venture agreement.

Avoid Personal Obligation

To accept a benefit is to sell one's liberty.

—Publilius Syrus

He who oweth is all in the wrong.

—Proverb

It is common for traveling American business executives and professionals upon arrival in a foreign country to be overwhelmed with hospitality and other courtesies provided by their foreign counterparts. Limousines and drivers may be made available, expensive parties arranged, lavish banquets laid out, and many sight-seeing opportunities offered. Often, gifts of significant value will be given. Go ahead and enjoy it. But bear in mind that all this lavish hospitality is intended to create obligation on a personal level, which it is hoped will cause you to make decisions favorable to your generous hosts (but which may or may not be in the best interests of you or your organization). Don't underestimate the effect these personal favors and gifts may have on the judgment of even the most aware recipient. The best response to this dilemma is not to reject the hospitality, but rather to reciprocate. For example, if a foreign company hosts you to a dinner at an expensive restaurant, schedule a dinner at which you are the host at the earliest appropriate occasion. By reciprocating the kindness and largess of your foreign friends, you avoid personal obligation. And you get two great dinners out of the deal. A neat solution all around.

Another agenda may also be playing itself out as your generous hosts fill nearly every minute of your stay with dinners, tours, meetings, shopping, and social calls. The more time they can control, the less chance you will have to discover alternatives or make other contacts. By controlling your activities, they have reduced your alternatives, which in turn reduces your negotiating leverage. Your active social schedule can also dissipate your strength, thereby weakening your ability to negotiate effectively. Pleading jet lag is often an acceptable defense. Keep in mind, however, that the most important part of the negotiation may not be bargaining in meetings but rather building a relationship through unpressured social interaction. Getting to know your counterparts is important. But so is your time, and you should use it to get done what you must, including rest and preparation.

Understand Emotions

As a man gets angry, he falls into error.

—Talmud

In a heated argument we lose sight of the truth.

—Publilius Syrus

The wise man has ordinary emotions, and therefore cannot respond to things without joy or sorrow. He responds to things, yet is not ensnared by them. It is wrong to say that because the wise man has no ensnarement, he therefore has no emotions.

—Wang Pi

Emotions vitally affect our ability to negotiate because every emotion brings with it an impetus to take action related to the emotion. These actions can be physical (such as flight from danger) or mental (such as the screening out of painful information). If we were experts at dissecting and explaining emotions, we would be writing the great American novel, not this modest book on negotiating. But we are not, and so we will limit our discourse on the subject to a few points as they affect negotiating.

In the context of your ability to negotiate effectively, emotions can affect: (1) your ability to communicate, and (2) your behavior and thus can be used to manipulate your actions. Each of us has emotional trigger points that clever negotiators can use to advance their objectives. Again, awareness is the key here. By becoming aware of our emotions, we can learn to change our reactions and avoid being manipulated (by others or by the emotions themselves). Becoming aware of your emotions can allow you to understand how feelings affect your ability to listen or understand the proposals of the other negotiator. Each of us has emotional filters that act to screen us from information we do not want to hear. If the emotion is directed against your negotiating counterpart, it may prevent you from empathizing and perceiving the other person's interests. While that may help you maintain your emotional state, it makes it tough to craft a deal that satisfies everyone. Awareness can break down these filters and allow us to see a situation or proposal as others do (or as it really is, if such an objective reality is knowable). The idea is to prevent the emotion from controlling the situation—a feat considerably easier to advise than to accomplish. At a minimum, awareness of the emotional dynamic of the negotiation can mitigate the most unconstructive consequences.

Nearly as counterproductive as being too affected by emotions is not feeling emotions at all. Emotions motivate us in all our roles, including that of negotiator. If you negotiate solely on the basis of logic, you miss emotional signals sent out by the other negotiator. Dante reserved the Ninth Circle of Hell for those who fail to make the most basic human connection: empathy. People who were incapable of connecting with other humans were relegated by Dante to a place in hell frozen over with ice. Negotiators who are incapable of empathy for the other negotiator may find themselves in an ice-filled negotiator's hell. You need to feel to understand. If you suppress your own feelings, you will be less capable of understanding the emotions of the other negotiator. The key is to be perceptive of feelings without being reactive. We call this approach to emotions in a negotiator "nonreactive empathy."

Anger is an emotion that is commonly felt by a negotiator dealing with other cultures. While we were soliciting anecdotes for this book, one relatively experienced businessman who does extensive business in Eastern Europe asked us, "Why does international negotiation have to be so difficult?" Why indeed? Life is difficult. Conflicts are bound to arise in any relationship. Once you recognize that the negotiating process is difficult, particularly so in a multicultural context, you begin to transcend the difficulty. You can strip away the unproductive anger and frustration and become more effective at reconciling interests and negotiating differences.

We know an executive of a mid-size apparel company who once received 50 bush hats from an Australian manufacturer. The hats were to be used on display models in department stores to promote his "Aussie" clothing line. When the hats arrived from Australia, they were black—the wrong color. He immediately dispatched a nasty facsimile to Sydney demanding the brown hats he had ordered. He learned in a return letter from the Australians that two shipments of hats had been switched by mistake. The Australians asked him to send the hats back to Australia by air freight so they could be exchanged for the hats sent to the other customer. He did so and waited a week for the brown hats to arrive. When, eventually, the box of hats arrived, he opened it and found 50 black hats. The executive was furious. He went into a rage and tore ten of the hats to shreds. The man's anger may have had some justification, but it was doing nothing to solve the problem. In fact, he had created a new problem since he had just bought ten black hats and had only forty hats to exchange for brown hats. His feelings of anger were understandable, but his manner of expressing those feelings was counterproductive.

Joseph Stalin was a master in the use of emotions. In meetings with U.S. and British negotiators over Allied assistance as the Nazis raced toward Moscow, Stalin alternated friendly and cordial discussions with hostile and adversarial outbursts. His emotional tactics threw the other negotiators off balance and helped strengthen a weak negotiating position. Stalin's skill was in using hot-cold emotional shifts to change the Soviets from supplicants to equal (and even morally superior) partners. Other Soviet leaders have exhibited this same tendency to shift from friendliness to hostility. The picture of Soviet Premier Khrushchev wearing a cowboy hat while visiting the United States taken shortly before the picture of him banging his shoe on the table during a speech graphically depicts this emotional polarity.

If the emotions in a negotiation are not yours, but rather are those of another negotiator, keeping emotions separate from the problem is probably best accomplished by providing that negotiator an opportunity to "let off steam." This can typically be done merely by allowing each party in turn to air his or her grievances or other emotions. Negotiators who are involved in an emotional dispute usually feel better when they have had an opportunity to vent their emotions. Particularly if one negotiator is at fault, allowing the aggrieved party to let out his or her anger or frustration is therapeutic to the relationship. If the negotiator who is guilty of the harmful conduct (whether or not it was intentional) acknowledges the error and apologizes, all the better. A well-timed and sincere apology can do wonders for resolving a dispute. Another significant benefit arises from "venting" or "grievance airing:" The desires of both sides have been further revealed, which should facilitate the search for a solution that meets both parties' needs.

Calling a recess in the negotiation can also help temper emotions (or demote tempers). In a play entitled *Private Lives*, Noel Coward created a couple who agreed that the shouting of the words "Solomon Isaacs" would immediately trigger a five-minute cooling-off period during which neither spouse could speak. Similar cooling-off periods, with or without the dramatic shouting of a code word, can be useful in an international negotiation. Seneca realized this when he wrote: "The greatest remedy for anger is delay."

Bringing in new negotiators from each side who are not emotionally involved in the dispute can also assist in reaching agreement. In the negotiations between Sony and Warner Communications in late 1989 regarding the release of producers

Peter Guber and Jon Peters from a five-year, exclusive distribution contract, a situation arose in which changing the negotiation team was deemed essential. The initial negotiation took place in the New York office of the infamous New York law firm of Skadden, Arps, Slate, Meagher & Flom. A number of representatives of Sony, including Walter Yetnikoff, were present. The Warner team was led by Time Inc. President Nicholas J. Nicholas and Arthur Liman, who gained fame as the special prosecutor in the Iran-Contra hearings. The atmosphere was hostile at the start and grew progressively more so. Eventually, a member of the Warner team became agitated with Yetnikoff, and yelled "[Expletive] you" at Yetnikoff, followed by a Bronx cheer.

As the negotiating session ended, Yetnikoff was slow to leave. Liman suspected him of trying to read documents the Warner team had left lying on the table, and confronted him: "Why are you the last to leave?" "[Expletive] you," Yetnikoff responded. Even Yetnikoff recognized his reaction was inappropriate. Yetnikoff is reported to have commented on the incident, "I was being jerky. It was . . . a very immature reaction." Sony realized that the hostility of Warner toward Yetnikoff made him a disruptive force in the negotiation and kept Yetnikoff out of the subsequent negotiating sessions. This had two effects. First, it facilitated a negotiated settlement between Sony and Warner. Second, it deprived Sony of Yetnikoff's counsel and experience during the negotiation, which many believe resulted in a settlement balanced heavily in Warner's favor.

Containing your negative emotions can be a difficult task in a heated negotiation. Warren Christopher, who gained fame for his role in the Iran hostage negotiations during the Carter administration, has been quoted as advising, "Never lose your temper—unless it's on purpose." It is even more difficult to keep your emotions in check if you decide to call a temporary or permanent halt to a relationship or negotiation. Try to avoid unconstructive behavior during the termination of a relationship. You may later regret critical statements made about the other side to third parties or the press when an opportunity (or need) later arises to do business with the same foreign company. Negative or hostile remarks made when negotiations are terminated achieve little and can cause long-term damage. Worse, you may do severe damage to your reputation. Given the importance of developing sound relationships in the course of global dealing, reputations tend to travel fast in the international community. Repairing a damaged reputation can be costly and difficult. It also pays to remember the adage, "Friends may come and go, but enemies accumulate."

Avoid Overnegotiation

More words count less.

—*Lao Tzu*

After hearing president Woodrow Wilson's speech revealing his Fourteen Points of Settlement that he proposed for inclusion in the treaty ending the First World War, French Prime Minister Clemenceau remarked, "Even God Almighty only has ten."

Americans tend to devote considerable energy to finely negotiating the terms of agreements. Provisions in contracts between Americans often attempt to deal with every possible contingency. Foreign businessmen generally tend to prefer more broadly framed agreements and to deal with the details of implementation as they arise. Conflicts resulting from these contrasting attitudes are nearly inevitable. The best approach to bridge these two attitudes about the proper nature and form of an agreement is to negotiate a more general agreement than would otherwise be acceptable. This shorter and more general agreement should create as much "continuing leverage" as possible for you. Focus on those issues of greatest importance and those most likely to affect the underlying relationship. Any international agreement should also contain mechanisms for resolving problems and disputes as they arise (for example, provisions that require mediation or arbitration). These mechanisms should be informal, private, and emphasize the speedy and inexpensive resolution of disputes.

Use a Team Approach and Choose the Right Players

The clever combatant looks to the effect of combined energy, and does not require too much from individuals. He takes individual talent into account, and uses each man according to his capabilities. He does not demand perfection from the untalented. When he utilizes combined energy, his fighting men become, as it were, like rolling logs or stones. The energy developed by good fighting men is as the momentum of a round stone rolled down a mountain thousands of feet in height.

—*Sun Tzu*

Americans typically prefer to use a small negotiating team or even one negotiator in their international dealings. Americans have adopted this "go it alone" attitude in many of history's most famous, and infamous, international negotiations. Some observers of international negotiations believe that Americans making this decision view themselves at some level to be the lone gunslinger or a U.S. marshal going out single-handed to eliminate a gang of outlaws. John Graham and Yoshihiro Sano describe what they call the John Wayne negotiation style:

Most American executives feel they should be able to handle any negotiation situation by themselves. "Four Japanese versus one American is no problem. I don't need any help. I can think and talk fast enough to get what I want, what the company needs."

Henry Kissinger commented on the John Wayne approach as follows:

I've always acted alone. Americans admire that enormously. Americans admire the cowboy leading the caravan, alone astride his horse. The cowboy entering . . . village or city alone on his horse.

Unfortunately, what works for Kissinger usually does not for merely mortal Americans.

The "lone negotiator" approach adopted by many American

negotiators may be explained in part by the high cost of international travel. While the out-of-pocket expenses incurred in sending a team of negotiators can be high, it may be much less than what is lost from an unsuccessful negotiation. Negotiations are particularly tiring and demanding when they take place in an international context. Tasks such as information collecting and analysis, strategy preparation, and bargaining can be divided among the various members of a team. Some of these tasks must be conducted concurrently during negotiations, making it difficult, if not impossible, for the solo negotiator to do justice to them all. Having other team members to rely on for psychological support or to critique your approaches can also be helpful.

Bringing a team to the negotiating table allows you to bring expertise to bear in each area under negotiation. This allows the lead negotiator to benefit from instant input in areas that may not be his or her specialty, such as engineering, tax, law, accounting, or marketing. Having a team behind you also provides you with the emotional support necessary to prevail. The fact that others are available to reassure you about your positions and performance can be important.

If possible, the people who will be dealing with the foreign company on a continuing basis should be part of the team that negotiates the initial agreement. If these people are involved in the negotiating process that results in the deal, they will be aware of the history of the negotiation as the need to interpret the agreement arises. Knowing how the negotiation progressed helps clarify what the parties had in mind when they drafted specific provisions of the agreement. The foreign company will not be able to claim later, for example, that the parties had some other informal side agreement or had a different view of the scope of a particular provision. Another important reason for including the day-to-day negotiators in the initial negotiation is that in many countries (particularly in Asia) promises made in a contract are viewed by many foreigners as having been made to the individuals involved in the negotiation. If the Americans implementing the agreement were not involved in the initial negotiation, their foreign counterparts may feel less bound to comply with its contractual requirements.

To expedite negotiations, it is often a good idea to bring both senior and junior employees to the negotiating table. Most people feel more compelled to comply with an agreement if the promises were made to a person rather than to a company. By having officials in each organization talk directly with their counterparts, this dynamic can be encouraged. In some cases it is helpful if separate negotiations among these individuals take place at different times or places.

In many countries, it is customary for the general principles of an agreement to be worked out by high-level officials and the details by more junior staff. However, it should be remembered that reaching an agreement on general principles is nearly always easier. While the big issues may ultimately be of greatest import, the greater ease with which they are typically resolved may be due to their higher level of generality. This allows each side to envision the implementation of the general principles in the manner most to their liking. From this human attribute springs Professor Parkinson's rule, "the time spent on any item of the agenda will be in inverse proportion to the sum involved." Whatever the reason, it always seems to be the small stuff that hangs up a deal.

The dynamic of team negotiations involving issues of status and authority can be subtle and complex. During a particular negotiation in Tokyo, three vice-presidents of an American financial services company found themselves up against five middle managers from a major Japanese trading company. Because of their egalitarian nature, the Americans naturally developed a casual working relationship with the Japanese, which reflected relative equality in status. The negotiations were progressing fairly well until two more senior executives and the president of the trading company joined the Japanese negotiating team. The arrival of these new participants completely disrupted the negotiations since no one of comparable status was present from the American company. Only the late arrival of a senior vice president from the United States who could deal with the senior Japanese negotiators as equals salvaged the negotiations.

Those who appreciate the value of a team approach to negotiation may seek to gain an advantage by isolating individuals of the other side from their team back-up. In his book *Years of Upheaval*, Henry Kissinger reveals that during the 1976 Nixon-Brezhnev summit, he received a 10 P.M. phone call from the Secret Service informing him that the general secretary was demanding that he meet immediately with the president. Brezhnev's demand came despite the fact that he had retired early from the day's negotiations on the pretext that he needed to rest for his trip the following day. Kissinger writes of this tactic: "It was a gross breach of protocol . . . It was also a transparent ploy to catch Nixon off-guard, and with luck to separate him from his advisers."

Of course, the power of numbers can be taken too far. Foreign companies sometimes go to great lengths to have at least a small numerical advantage in the size of their negotiating team. We have a friend who was involved in some rather lengthy and complex debt-rescheduling negotiations in Poland. As issues were raised, various experts were brought in from the United States. Each day when he entered the conference room in a Warsaw government ministry, he noticed the most senior Polish bureaucrat counting the number of American negotiators who entered the room. He would then use the telephone to contact some unknown associate. Additional Polish negotiators would then arrive to precisely balance the number of Americans present. One morning, late in the negotiation, the Americans arrived with far more negotiators than was usual. The Pole made his call but appeared quite upset. He slammed down the telephone and waited for three more Polish negotiators to appear. The Americans still had a three-man numerical advantage and the Polish bureaucrats were visibly displeased. The first order of business for the day was negotiating a limit in the size of each country's negotiating team. Only after three Americans left the room did the original agenda commence. While numerical superiority can create an advantage, there are limits to how many negotiators should be on a team. As numbers rise, the team structure eventually becomes unworkable. As with most things in life, balance is called for.

Part of preparing for a negotiation should itself involve a type of subnegotiation within your own team. Our interviews repeatedly revealed that foreign-based managers spent almost as much time negotiating with the home office as negotiating with outside parties.

AT&T is one U.S. company that learned the hard way about the importance of a unified team approach. In a 1987 negotiation to purchase the telephone maker Cie Generale des Construc-tions Telephoniques owned by the French government, AT&T organized two separate managing teams, one located in New York and the other located in the Netherlands. The two groups often worked at cross-purposes and wasted energy trying to establish which group had responsibility for which issues. The U.S. government also tried to directly intervene on behalf of AT&T in the negotiation, creating further confusion. Robert Dalziel, President of AT&T's Brussels subsidiary, was quoted in the *Wall Street Journal* as saying, "We would have been dumb not to have learned some lessons from those [failed French] negotiations." When an opportunity arose later to enter the Italian telephone exchange manufacturing market, AT&T es-tablished a single negotiating team. The team was able to draw on the support of a 20 person office staffed by Italians. The U.S. government was involved in the effort, but with clear instructions that only the single AT&T team had authority to negotiate the deal. While the negotiations were difficult and lasted well over a year, the process was facilitated greatly by properly assigning the negotiation authority to a single team working toward a common goal.

During a long transatlantic flight, one of the authors listened to an English diplomat describe a recent conference he had attended at the United Nations. Each country except Japan and West Germany had sent a delegation of approximately ten members headed by a chief delegate. The Japanese delegation consisted of over 100 delegates. A few days into the conference, the Englishman learned that five different Japanese ministries could not agree on who was responsible for the conference, so each ministry had sent 20 individuals to the conference. The Japanese delegation had five chief delegates who fought among each other incessantly. The West Germans also had an inter-ministry dispute and had agreed that every ministry would send five delegates. Each German ministry was allowed to se-lect the chief delegate for two weeks of the six-week conference.

The Englishman described the result of the conference for both the Japanese and West German delegations as disastrous. The Japanese delegation had little influence because it could not present a unified position and the West German delegation was ineffective because decisions and policies changed as the chief delegate changed. It is reassuring sometimes to hear stories of international ineptitude involving nationalities other than the United States.

One way to avoid this sort of divided team approach is to designate a team leader. This leader should be accountable for the outcome of the negotiation to the appropriate person in the organizational hierarchy, and this should be understood by the other team members. While this leader must be the primary decision maker for the team, she does not need to make all presentations. If another member of the team needs to address certain issues, he should be requested to do so by the leader. The leader must maintain control, however, or the personal agendas of the individual team members can take over. An effective team leader will be able to focus the attention of the negotiators on the relationship between the two teams and not the many relationships among the team members. Between two teams each having two members there are seven possible relationships (A-B, A-C, A-D, B-C, B-D, C-D, and Team 1 versus Team 2). As the number of participants rises, the number of relationships with which the parties must deal rises geometrically. Only if the leader maintains control of the process by focusing the team's attention on the primary relationship can the team's agenda be advanced.

In selecting the right negotiators, Americans often make the mistake of changing the lead negotiator or members of the negotiating team too often. The importance of maintaining continuity tends to be appreciated to a greater extent by foreigners than by Americans. This reflects the relatively greater importance that most foreigners assign to the relationships involved. When American companies change negotiators often, they convey a message that they are unreliable and disorganized. Changing team members during a negotiation can result in a loss of continuity and set back progress toward agreement. At the very least, the identity of the team leader should remain constant throughout the negotiation. At some points in a negotiation the only thing keeping it going is the momentum of the process. Altering the composition of a negotiating team can kill that momentum. One of the authors was involved in a negotiation between a U.S. and a Japanese company that began to take on the character of the perpetual wars in George Orwell's 1984. Comic relief was provided by the constantly changing composition of the U.S. team. No two negotiating sessions featured exactly the same lineup. Had the U.S. company not been absorbed in a takeover, it eventually might have rotated every one of its executives through this team. When former executives of the U.S. company get together, they probably still talk about the difficulties they encountered in their marathon negotiations with the Japanese.

While a stable negotiating team can facilitate the negotiation process when progress is being made, changing the composition of the negotiating team may actually be beneficial if a genuine deadlock is encountered. Changing team members in a deadlock allows new brainstorming to occur, as well as creating an opportunity to abandon positions previously staked out. The best response to negotiators frozen in position because of concerns about face or honor can be to bring in new negotiators focused on reconciling interests to create mutual benefit.

A number of studies have been performed in an attempt to determine the most important characteristics in a negotiator. Throughout the centuries, the attributes that constitute the ideal negotiator have remained fairly constant. A veteran negotiator described the attributes of a skilled negotiator at another place in time as follows:

The complete negotiator, according to seventeenth and eighteenth century manuals on diplomacy, should have a quick mind but unlimited patience, know how to dissemble without being a liar, inspire trust without trusting others, be modest but assertive, charm others without succumbing to their charm, and possess plenty of money and a beautiful wife while remaining indifferent to all temptations of riches and women. Today, of course, the star negotiator may herself be a wife.

Among the more important attributes of a successful negotiator are:

- Patience
- Communication skills
- Persistence
- Flexibility
- Tact
- Open-mindedness
- Subject knowledge
- Willingness to take risks
- Physical stamina
- Self-confidence
- Decisiveness
- Creativity
- Willingness to listen
- Self-control
- Long-range outlook
- Persistence
- Sensitivity to interests and needs of others

If you find your self-esteem plummeting as you come up short on variable after variable, don't worry. The comprehensiveness of the list assures that no single person is going to score high on all the desired traits. (On the other hand, if you consider yourself strong in all these areas, you should probably reassess your humility.)

Use Pauses to Deliberate and Consult

The right word may be effective but no word was ever as effective as the mightily timed pause.

—*Mark Twain*

Abraham Lincoln commanded a platoon of Bucktail Rangers during the Black Hawk War. Captain Lincoln was marching his men in formation toward their objective when he encountered a fence and a narrow gate. Since Lincoln had no formal military training, he did not know the proper command that would allow his men to pass through the barrier. Lincoln ordered the platoon to halt, thought about the problem, and then issued his order. "Company dismissed for two minutes. At the end of that time, fall in and on the other side of the fence."

Just as Lincoln discovered in his military experience, scheduling a properly timed break or adjournment can be beneficial in negotiations. Pauses in the negotiation can allow you to formulate strategy, assess progress, obtain information or instructions, and, no less important, rest and recuperate. A pause can also remove circumstances that have resulted in an impasse. A change in the composition of the other negotiating team or the loss or addition of alternatives are two examples of circumstances that might call for an adjournment to reevaluate the negotiation.

Breaks in the negotiation can also give the foreign negotiators sufficient time to understand and become comfortable with your proposals. During the Paris peace talks to end the Vietnam War, because both sides needed time to analyze and understand proposals made by the other side, the negotiations involved more breaks than actual negotiating sessions. One can only speculate whether the breaks actually expedited those painfully slow talks.

When an American company is negotiating an agreement in a non-English-speaking country, its negotiators may be at a significant disadvantage. This is particularly true if no American in the negotiating team speaks the language of the foreign country. As the negotiations are taking place and strategy needs to be formulated, the foreign executives have the advantage of being able to shift into a language that the Americans do not understand. This allows the foreign negotiators to formulate proposals and reach a consensus on important issues in the privacy of their native tongue without ever leaving the room. It also allows the lead negotiator to request input and technical data from subordinates or input from professional advisers such as lawyers or accountants and receive confidential responses. Americans who do not speak the foreign language do not have this same advantage and as a result must insist that they be able to leave the room to discuss important policy matters before making a proposal or offering a response. Having even a single person on your negotiating team who understands the foreign language will go a long way toward solving this problem. One of the authors has been able on several occasions to use some modest conversational Japanese language ability to convince the Japanese negotiators across the table that their private conversations are not entirely secure. Often it's enough just to create a credible doubt in their minds. Having a single team member who speaks the language does not completely overcome the handicap. Such a person typically will have a real opportunity to relay to his fellow negotiators what is being said in the foreign language only after the negotiation or during a break. If it is vital that this information be made available to the American team during the negotiation, it is certainly advisable to call a pause in the proceedings for a strategy session.

Hiring a national of the foreign country to attend the negotiations can be helpful in lessening the language disadvantage. However, care should be taken in hiring this individual since she may consider herself to be a citizen of the foreign country first, and an employee of the American company second. Art Buchwald had this in mind when he wrote, part in jest and part in truth: "Never trust a man who speaks the language of the country where he is stationed." This monitor may even be contacted outside of the negotiation and offered a monetary or other incentive to collaborate with the foreign company. In other words, the monitor may put her interests or the interests of her own country ahead of your interests. There may be nothing more sinister about this than simply human nature. A monitor may also be reluctant or unwilling to speak openly to you because of social constraints unknown to you.

Our experience has revealed another similar linguistic (or nationalistic) pitfall. There seems to be a fairly common tendency to assume that someone on the other side who speaks English particularly well or has spent considerable time in the United States is, if not actually an ally, at least a sympathetic intermediary. One of the authors, while representing a major Japanese trading company in long, complex negotiations in

Osaka with a U.S. company, found the Americans seeking out his insight on the Japanese and his recommendations as to how best to deal with them. Despite his repeated reminders that he represented the Japanese company, the Americans came to regard him as if he were their attorney on the deal and would insist on sharing all their strategy and tactics with him. The Americans, all senior executives, were nonetheless inexperienced with negotiating in Japan and seemed desperately to need help and reassurance. They may have been reassured but they were probably not helped.

Ask Questions

It is in the answers to questions that knowledge consists.

—Aristotle

Questions are never indiscreet. Answers sometimes are.

—Oscar Wilde

It is better to know some of the questions than all of the answers.

—James Thurber

Does anyone have questions for my answers?

—Henry Kissinger

More effective than telling someone something is asking them something. Answering a question gives the other negotiator an opportunity to feel in control as well as to unload. To help draw the other negotiator out, trying using questions beginning with "what," rather than "why." "Why" demands a linear response. It implies a cause and effect and calls for judgment. "What," on the other hand, is descriptive. It calls for a contextual response that comprehends the whole. "Why" is confrontational; "what" is cooperative. If you seek to intimidate or disarm the other negotiator, confront him with a series of "why" questions. But if you seek information with which to craft a mutually beneficial outcome, stick to "what" questions.

Questions uncover information that you can use to discover interests. You can then formulate value-creating solutions based on these interests. Asking the proper questions cannot only result in new opportunities for mutual gain but can be an excellent persuasive tool. One technique for persuading through questioning is to take the statement that you would use to build your argument, think up questions to which those statements are answers, and then ask the questions. People who do most of the talking are also more apt to view a proposal as their idea. The proper questions can provide you with information that can be used in formulating strategy, assessing the value of a settlement, or in correcting erroneous assumptions.

When answering your question, the opposing negotiator is forced to examine the premises upon which her position rests. Often, these premises are flawed, and this will be revealed in the weakness of her answer. The Marquis de Vauvenargues wrote: "When an idea is too weak to support a simple statement, it is a sign that it should be rejected." In this way, poor answers to your questions can lead the other negotiator to back off from a demand or otherwise moderate positions.

To increase the flow of information, take notes. People convey more information when they believe you find what they say is valuable enough to write down. (The exception to this is when what is being shared is particularly sensitive or confidential.) You convey the message that they are important and that you are interested in them. This helps you build the relationship necessary to maximize the result of the negotiation. It is often wise to ask the same question more than once during the course of a negotiation. The second answer can provide new information or reveal a previously unrecognized misunderstanding. Questions can also provide you with an opportunity to avoid answering the other side's questions. For example, when you are confronted with a question you would rather not answer, answer the question with another question. Asking a question can also be a good response when the other side makes a demand in the form of an ultimatum.

Information is always a precious commodity in business, but it is especially so when you are involved in an international negotiation. The costs of information gathering as well as the risk of obtaining false or inaccurate information are much greater in an unfamiliar environment. Information should be gradually revealed to the other side as the negotiation progresses. Once information is allowed to escape, it cannot be recalled. The Japanese have a saying, "You are made strong by what you withhold, and weak by what you reveal." As information goes out, it should be matched by a reverse flow of information from the foreign negotiators. Hopefully, a climate of cooperative reciprocity can be established during this process of exchanging information. When another negotiator makes an inquiry, don't forget that not all questions deserve an answer. Americans typically have difficulty not answering questions and sophisticated foreigners tend to be aware of this cultural trait. You should learn to answer questions without revealing information before it is time.

A typical battle over information occurs when an American buyer arrives in a foreign country to purchase products. In most cases, the American will immediately reveal his requirements. A purchaser of women's dresses, for example, might desperately need 100 dozen silk dresses in New York by October. If the American buyer reveals that his receipt of the dresses is necessary to save his business, before determining the seller's ability to deliver the dresses, the seller is able to demand a premium in return for meeting the buyer's delivery requirement. The usual claim of the seller is that his factories are at full capacity and that only a premium price or better terms can guarantee delivery. The American buyer should determine the seller's capacity to deliver the dresses before he reveals his requirements. In an interest-based negotiation, the exchange of information by the negotiators should be reciprocal. This produces both trust and momentum toward a mutually beneficial result.

Be Silent

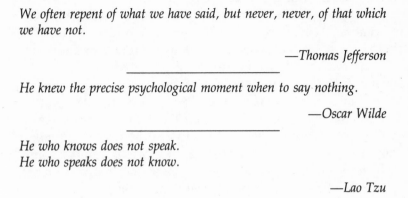

We often repent of what we have said, but never, never, of that which we have not.

—*Thomas Jefferson*

He knew the precise psychological moment when to say nothing.

—*Oscar Wilde*

He who knows does not speak.
He who speaks does not know.

—*Lao Tzu*

Americans are particularly uncomfortable with silence. If conversation during a negotiation ceases for any reason (such as when a foreign negotiator stops to mentally formulate a response or a new inquiry), Americans typically become uncomfortable. Their discomfort usually causes them to begin speaking. In so doing, they may be revealing more than might be prudent, if not actually ceding on points unnecessarily. Moreover, by filling every conversational gap, one may deprive the foreigner of an opportunity to speak and thereby reveal more about his needs and goals. Don't negotiate with yourself. Be patient and wait for a response to your comments, proposals, and offers.

Americans also habitually interrupt foreigners by finishing their sentences or interjecting their own opinion while the foreigner is still speaking. Americans most often interrupt a speaker when they disagree with the speaker's opinion. This behavior is not only rude but also deprives you of the opportunity to acquire valuable information. Of course, Americans are not alone in their tendency to interrupt others. During an after-dinner conversation, Winston Churchill's son Randolph was trying to make a point when his father interrupted him to express his own opinion. Randolph listened for a few seconds and then attempted to bring the conversation back to his own line of reasoning. The prime minister's response was swift and curt: "Don't interrupt me when I am interrupting!" If the foreign negotiator is struggling to find the right English word to convey his meaning, by all means let him find his own way. Your suggested word or words may not be what he had in mind at all. Too often, the foreigner will agree with your word choice out of embarrassment, politeness, or lack of knowledge.

If a period of silence occurs during a negotiation, bite your tongue! If that sounds too painful, breathe through your nose or in some other manner that keeps your mouth shut. Remaining silent when the foreigner has taken an unreasonable position or given an ultimatum can also be useful in a negotiation. Let your silence make him uncomfortable. His discomfort with the silence may cause him to suggest a more reasonable approach. Americans tend to feel some sense of personal responsibility for an awkward silence. Many foreigners are aware of this American tendency and, accordingly, will stop speaking intentionally to elicit additional information or concessions from the American. Try using this tactic yourself. A good rule of thumb is that it is never appropriate to speak unless you can improve the silence.

Countergamesmanship

There is a vast difference between games and play. Play is played for fun, but games are deadly serious and you do not play them to enjoy yourself.

—*Maurice Baring*

Games always cover something deep and intense, else there would be no excitement in them, no pleasure, no power to stir us.

—*Antoine de Saint-Exupery*

Gamesmanship embraces the range of tactics, often ethically or intellectually improper, used to achieve unilateral advantage in a negotiation. Skilled gamesmen will use a variety of ploys to shift the negotiating situation to their favor. Some form of gamesmanship is encountered in any negotiation. International negotiations are no exception. Before a tactic can be developed for countering a particular form of gamesmanship, you must first recognize the negotiating ploy you have encountered. This is not always easy as the tactics of an experienced gamesman can be subtle. Recognizing when gamesmanship is being utilized is also useful since most ploys can be turned on the other negotiator for your advantage. As a rule, those negotiators who avoid using gamesmanship and instead utilize a principled negotiation approach will be most successful. However, even a principled negotiator may occasionally be forced to engage in countergamesmanship to achieve a mutually beneficial outcome.

With regard to gamesmanship, remember that all the clever skills, psychological ploys, and other tricks of negotiating will probably prove worthless if the other negotiator has an alternative you can't top. We are reminded of the scene in Steven Spielberg's *Raiders of the Lost Ark* in which Indiana Jones is confronted by an attacker brandishing swords with amazing skill. That skill proved useless, however, when Indy pulled his revolver from its holster and dispatched the attacker with a single shot.

Brinksmanship

If you are scared to go to the brink, you are lost.

—*John Foster Dulles*

ULTIMATUM, n. *In diplomacy, a last demand before resorting to concessions.*

—*Ambrose Bierce*

Brinksmanship describes the practice of making demands that force the other negotiator to the limit of his or her ability to concede before stopping. One of the most common forms of brinksmanship is an ultimatum. Brinksmanship was used successfully by Mexico in 1982 during one of the many negotiations with the United States over Mexico's foreign debt. The Mexican negotiators were led by Finance Minister Jesus Silva Herzog. Federal Reserve Board Chairman Paul Volcker and Treasury Secretary Donald Regan headed the U.S. team. After several days of talks to avert a default on Mexico's foreign debt of $82 billion, a near settlement had been reached that included a multibillion dollar financial rescue package and huge purchases of Mexican oil for the U.S. Strategic Petroleum Reserve. The only sticking point was the demand by the United States for a $100 million "negotiating fee" (a diplomatic way for Mexico to pay interest without incurring political damage). Finance Minister Herzog asked then Mexican President Lopez Portillo how to respond to the U.S. demand for a negotiating fee. Portillo considered the demand and is reported to have ordered Herzog to respond, "Let Rome burn." When the United States considered the potentially disastrous effect of a financial collapse in its southern neighbor, the demand for a negotiation fee was halved to $50 million. The Mexicans agreed and the financial bailout was successful.

One form of brinksmanship that is particularly difficult to deal with is the *fait accompli* approach. In technical terms a *fait accompli* reduces the number of possible decisions by eliminating certain alternatives. A *fait accompli* in military terms can be considered the equivalent of a preemptive strike. When executed properly, preemption will eliminate the preferred alternatives of the other negotiator and leave only the alternatives that you desire (assuming, of course, that these are mutually exclusive). Take the case of two farmers traveling toward each other on tractors on a one-lane road. Each wants the other to pull off the road and let him pass so he can get home sooner. As the tractors near each other, one farmer chooses to use a *fait accompli* approach. He removes the steering wheel and throws it into the trailer he is towing. The other farmer is left with the choice of either pulling over or colliding with the other tractor. His only real choice is to pull off the road.

One oft-cited example of the use of *fait accompli* occurred when the United States acted in 1955 to organize the Southeast Asia Treaty Organization (SEATO) without consulting its major ally, Great Britain, which still had colonial interests in the region. The action of the United States presented Great Britain with SEATO on a "take it or leave it" basis. Britain was left with the choice of accepting the alliance as it stood, or rejecting it altogether. The former was clearly the preferred alternative, even if it meant acquiescing to the U.S. plan.

The *fait accompli* approach was employed less successfully in 1989 when Sony tapped producers Peter Guber and Jon Peters to head Columbia Pictures, which it was in the process of acquiring. An employment agreement was reached with Guber and Peters, the producers of *Batman*, notwithstanding the dynamic duo's exclusive five-year production agreement with Warner. When the *fait accompli* was presented to Warner head Steve Ross, he was furious. The resulting negotiations to obtain Warner's release of Guber and Peters resulted in a deal reportedly worth from $500 million to $1 billion for Warner. Many people in the motion picture industry believe that if the producers had approached Warner before they signed the deal with Sony and humbly asked for a release, Steve Ross would have granted it. An investment banker who is a close adviser of Ross and who was a key player at the negotiations with Sony, said later, "I think there would have been a much different outcome had Jon Peters and Peter Guber come to Warner before their commitments with Columbia and Sony. I suspect it would have lacked the level of unhappiness that both parties have had."

A major risk in using the *fait accompli* approach is that it may evoke irrational behavior whereby the other negotiator chooses a mutually undesirable outcome as the preferred alternative in order to inflict punishment or exact retribution. In almost all cases, a *fait accompli* approach is harmful to the relationship and may preclude mutually beneficial outcomes.

Brinksmanship has been known to be employed in the hospitality industry, when an established hotel is filling its rooms and profiting handsomely from a tight market. To forestall new entry into the market, the established hotel will announce plans for a new hotel or a major expansion of the existing one. Typically, an architect is engaged and permits are applied for. After the announcement is made, further activity on the expansion plans tends to be directly proportional to signs that someone else is also considering building a new hotel.

Another form of brinksmanship involves using the need of the other negotiator to reach an agreement by a certain date to your advantage. A common setting for this tactic is when one negotiator is negotiating in a foreign country and the date of his or her plane reservation home is rapidly approaching. This tactic was attempted on a buyer for a major American retailer who was negotiating in Brazil to purchase a large quantity of shoes. As he entered the lobby of his hotel, he noticed an employee of the Brazilian firm hand an envelope to the concierge. The buyer's suspicions were that the employee had paid a bribe for information on the length of his hotel reservation. The buyer called the airline and confirmed that many seats remained for the days following his departure. He then called his office and delayed his departure by two days. A contingency reservation was also made at another hotel in São Paulo. As the buyer's departure date approached, the smiles and demands of the Brazilians evaporated. Concessions rolled in at an ever-increasing rate. The buyer left Brazil with his best purchase price ever and on schedule. As was the case in *Hamlet*, the Brazilians were "hoist by their own petard." In effect, they were defeated by the same tactic that they meant to use to defeat the American buyer.

Another example of brinksmanship occurred during negotiations between U.S. and Japanese computer companies. The U.S. computer company was a world leader in terms of technology and was dominant in both U.S. and European marketplaces. However, the U.S. company had not been successful in entering the Japanese market. Negotiations with the Japanese company concerned the establishment of a separate Japanese company that would be responsible for localizing the technology and conducting the necessary marketing activities in Japan. The negotiations between the two companies had gone on for nearly a year and the responsible executives from the U.S. company believed they were relatively close to agreement. The parties had spent literally hundreds of hours negotiating all aspects of the contract.

When the Americans felt they had nearly reached an agreement, they invited executives from the Japanese company to the United States to "tie down the final details." The Japanese arrived on a Monday, and during the course of the week everything seemed to be proceeding smoothly. On Thursday evening, the president of the U.S. company announced that an elaborate banquet would be held in honor of the Japanese guests during which the final agreements would be signed. The chairman of the U.S. computer company, who had not been directly involved in the negotiations after the initial stages, was to be the host of the banquet. On Friday morning, when the parties met to discuss what the Americans felt were minor details, the Japanese executives announced that they could not accept several points that had previously been agreed upon. These points concerned major issues, including whether the U.S. company had an option to purchase a controlling interest, how "in-kind" investments by the Japanese would be valued, and how the U.S. company's technology would be protected by the Japanese company.

The Americans who were negotiating that Friday were astounded and perplexed. However, they knew that the chairman of their company was expecting to sign the agreement that evening. As the day progressed, the Americans became more and more nervous and began to make concessions. By late afternoon the Japanese had obtained every concession they had demanded except one. Worsening the negotiating position of the American company was the fact that as the day wore on, numerous members of its team excused themselves from the meeting because they had "made plans for the weekend." This meant that the number of American negotiators decreased steadily until finally only two Americans remained at 7:00 P.M. The banquet had been scheduled to begin at 6:30, and the Japanese were intransigent. Finally, at 7:30 the chairman called the senior American negotiator and demanded to know where his guests were. The last concession was quickly made by the Americans and a deal was reached. As passive observers of this dynamic, we were left stunned in disbelief. The Americans had an agreement but not the bargain they expected. The Japanese obtained more than they could have dreamed from the negotiation.

Of course, American negotiators have also been known to use the pressure of a deadline to obtain concessions. Representatives of a U.S. electronics company came to Seoul to negotiate the final outstanding issues in a major joint-venture agreement. There were fundamental differences in the approach of the two parties. The Americans viewed the joint-venture company as a cost center to provide a needed component at a competitive price. The Korean party viewed the project as an entry into a new and lucrative market. Despite these differences, a successful negotiation had reduced the outstanding issues to a short list of specific, but important, details.

Upon arrival in Seoul, the Americans were presented with a written schedule for their stay in Korea: Negotiate from 10:00 A.M. to 12:30 P.M. Lunch. Negotiate from 2:00 until 5:00. Return to hotel and rest. Meet at 6:30 for dinner and reveling at the Kisaeng House. The Korean parties had a sincere desire to entertain their guests, but they also knew that this would aid in their taking control of the negotiations. At 5:00 P.M., the Koreans wanted to break, in accordance with the schedule. The Americans expressed a desire to continue for a while as a number of issues remained to be addressed. Not wishing to insult them, the Korean side acquiesced. As time passed, the Koreans became tired and hungry (Koreans, like the authors of this book, cannot tolerate missing a meal). The Americans were not tired and pressed on. "Let's finish our business first, then we will really be able to celebrate," they said. As the Korean representatives became impatient, they agreed more readily to the suggestions presented by the American side.

Finally, one of the Americans went forward and listed on a blackboard the issues that were unresolved. One by one they tackled them. When one of the Koreans came up with an acceptable solution, the American who was now "moderating" the discussion handed him the eraser and sent him up to eliminate that one. It became quite a game and resulted in a speedy resolution of the remaining items. The important point here is that the Koreans did not feel that they were being unfairly pressured, since their willingness to capitulate was self-generated.

Often the best way to deal with brinksmanship in the form of an ultimatum is to ignore the demand and direct the discussion in another area. Asking questions about the assumptions on which the ultimatum is based may also be an effective technique to counter brinksmanship. You can also attack the nature of the ultimatum rather than its substance. Ultimately, however, the use of an ultimatum forces you to consider your Best Alternative To a Negotiated Agreement (BATNA). If you do not have a BATNA, you may be in serious trouble if you encounter this form of brinksmanship. It is therefore crucial that all potential alternatives to the proposal under negotiation be identified during the preparation stage well before an ultimatum arises. And if you consider resorting to brinksmanship yourself, remember: *Never* present an ultimatum if you're not prepared to follow through with it.

Two Bites at the Apple

A fool is cheated both coming and going.

—Proverb

If the foreign negotiator does not have decision-making authority and the negotiated terms must be sent to a final decision maker for approval, an opportunity has been created to demand additional concessions. This situation results in "two bites at the apple." Most of us have encountered this tactic when negotiating over an auto purchase; the salesperson always seems to require the manager's approval for the deal you propose, as if he doesn't know the limit of his authority.

It is always important to determine whether the other negotiator has final decision-making authority. This determination should be made by contacting outside sources as well as inquiring directly with the other negotiator. Remember that a negotiator may be pretending to have less decision-making power than she actually possesses. This fiction allows the negotiator to save face if her authority is revoked. The tactic also permits her to use her ambiguous authority to advantage by creating a two-tiered approval structure.

One of our clients was involved in a protracted negotiation with a French business executive. Every time the client made a new proposal, the Frenchman would would pick up the telephone and call a colleague. A discussion in French would ensue that would last from two to ten minutes. After the conversation, the Frenchman would give his answer on the proposal. This process continued through several days of negotiation and was quite annoying. The two Frenchmen had talked by telephone at least twenty times. The client finally became so frustrated with the French negotiator's lack of decision-making authority that he remarked, when the Frenchman was again reaching for the telephone, "Does the person you keep calling speak English?" The Frenchman answered, "But of course." "Then why don't you just give me the telephone and let's get on with this." The remark was not particularly diplomatic and could have resulted in an avoidable confrontation. But it did reflect the difficulty of negotiating with a person who has no decision-making authority.

A friend of the authors' tells the following story about the two bites at the apple approach:

The perennial problem in negotiating in Korea is locally referred to as the "Mr. Big" ploy. The foreign team comes to Korea and meets with their Korean counterparts to discuss technical, financial, and legal issues. Draft agreements are revised and final execution copies are prepared. At this point, the Koreans reveal that they must take the agreement to the "chairman" for his approval. Instantly, what was perceived as a final agreement is only tentative. While the American negotiators had full authority to cut the deal, they find that their counterparts did not.

So into the meeting walks Mr. Big. All the Koreans bow low, and the Americans don't know how to react. The status of the foreign negotiators has already been defined by the earlier negotiations. They have no one left to bring in as Mr. Big's counterpart. Mr. Big looks over the agreement, tosses out what he doesn't like, changes the royalty rate and term, board composition, voting requirements, guarantee provisions, dividend policy, etcetera, and expects all the lower echelon personnel—American and Korean—to accept his superior wisdom.

Occasionally this ploy works and the foreign party agrees to unacceptable compromises just to avoid having wasted the entire time spent in negotiation. In other cases, it throws the entire negotiation process into chaos and results in the foreign representatives returning without a signed agreement and basically having to start over again. The moral here is to understand the local customs concerning corporate authority and to pin down the degree of authority that the negotiators actually have. Often they use persons who are skilled in English but who have little real authority. If major items require a higher-level approval, insist that the responsible person be present or that the active negotiators go to him for approval before moving on to other issues that may depend on the major points.

Various means can be employed to counter this tactic. One is to state at the outset that if any agreement reached between those persons present at the negotiation is subject to review by more senior officers or officials, and these officers demand concessions or modifications, then the entire agreement is subject to renegotiation. Alternatively you might insist that the foreign decision maker be present during the negotiation. For small American companies this is not always possible because of a lack of negotiating leverage. We have found that the most effective approach is to hold out your own "Mr. Big" (or "Mrs. Big" as the case may be) by informing the foreign negotiators that the final decision maker for your company is not present (even if he or she is). We make it a practice always to keep the final decision maker on our side out of the detailed negotiations in order to preserve our flexibility to defer agreement on troubling points and to counter the "two bites at the apple" tactic if it is employed by the other side.

The importance of finding the decision maker does not mean that lower-level employees can be ignored; as a general rule, it is not a good idea to alienate the functionaries. Though minions may not be decision makers, they are often in a position to kill or seriously delay the deal if they feel they have been bypassed or made to lose face. In other words, they may not be able to say "yes" but they can say "no." Thus, in most countries, proposals generally should proceed through proper channels (that is, through the lower-level employees) to reach the decision maker, even if this procedure may appear to result in some degree of delay. In the end, this path may in fact be more expedient.

A classic two bites at the apple situation arises when an agreement must be submitted for the approval of the foreign government before it can be implemented. In many countries, a private company and its government are in collusion to achieve a common goal. An example of such a situation occurred when the president of a major multinational manufacturer was negotiating to license its technology to a company in Malaysia. After several weeks of bargaining, the two companies were deadlocked over the appropriate royalty rate. The Malaysia firm was demanding a royalty of three percent of net sales and the multinational seven percent. A "solution" was found when the multinational agreed to provide certain know-how without charge in return for the Malaysian firm's accepting a seven percent royalty. The license agreement was then submitted to the Malaysian government for its required approval. One of its conditions for granting the approval was that the parties agree on a royalty rate of three percent of net sales. In effect, the multinational received nothing for its concession on know-how.

Another two bites at the apple situation occurs when the other negotiator agrees to your proposal but then introduces entirely new demands. This tactic was used by Maltese negotiators during negotiations over rent payable for the British naval base on the island. The Maltese prime minister repeatedly agreed to the British proposals but always introduced new demands. "Yes, that is fine, but we need a ten million pound development loan," the Maltese would say. Since no real strategic alternative to the naval base at Malta existed, the British were forced to make repeated concessions. Often the best response to this "Yes, but . . ." style of negotiation is to inform the other negotiator that all issues must be renegotiated if a new issue is introduced. An indirect way of doing the same thing is to simply reopen bargaining on previously settled issues or introduce new issues of your own. Either way, the message should be sent that upsetting the preexisting balance of the agreement requires negotiation of a new balance.

False Desires, Demands, or Facts

He pretends not to clinch the deal while going to fetch the precision scale.

—*Malagasy Proverb*

Diplomacy is the art of letting someone else have your way.

—*Daniele Vare*

In his classic book *Uncle Remus, His Songs and Sayings*, Joel Chandler Harris tells the story in which Brer Rabbit is captured by a fox. As the fox is contemplating how to kill his prize, Brer Rabbit begins to negotiate:

I don't care what you do with me, so long as you don't fling me in that brier-patch. Roast me, but don't fling me in that brier-patch. . . . Drown me just as deep as you please, but don't fling me in that brier-patch. . . . Skin me, snatch out my eyeballs, tear out my ears by the roots, and cut off my legs, but don't fling me in that brier-patch.

The fox gleefully chooses the alternative he believes the rabbit fears most and, by throwing the rabbit in the brier patch, allows him to escape. A clever negotiator is often able to gain an advantage by making the other side aware of a false desire. This form of gamesmanship is quite difficult to pull off successfully. The fox just may choose to roast you, drown you, or . . . well, you get the picture. For this reason, the Brer Rabbit approach is best used on foxes and other ignorant, careless, or vindictive negotiators.

The practice of making false demands is similar to the Brer Rabbit approach. A false demand is usually made when you learn during information gathering that the other negotiator badly wants something that is of little or no value to you. In such a situation, you can by subterfuge create a bargaining chip that need not necessarily have existed. For example, companies from developing countries often desire to control domestic distribution of products produced under a royalty-bearing license agreement. American firms often have little desire to do business in the country other than collecting the royalty. To create a bargaining chip, an American firm might initially demand control over distribution of the goods produced under the license in the foreign country. Later, in return for other concessions, the American company can agree to relinquish control over domestic distribution.

Making a false demand or indicating a false desire can allow you to take advantage of a bargaining technique known as "packaging." In using this tactic, you might say, "We will give you rights to distribute the product in your country if you concede on our price and delivery concerns." Be careful, however, that in employing the packaging approach you do not reveal the importance you place on obtaining any given item under negotiation.

The major risk in revealing false desires or making false demands is that you may realize an unintended result. As a case in point, the other company in the above example may decide that handling distribution is unprofitable and accept your offer. Massive loss of face may be entailed if you are forced to back off from your deception.

It is always wise to examine the validity of factual assertions made by a foreign negotiator. False facts often take the form of a statement from a foreign negotiator that the host government requires a certain provision or certain terms. A good example is a foreign negotiator's assertion that only a royalty of less than five percent is acceptable to the government. You should never accept this type of statement without independently confirming its validity. Often the best sources of confirmation of the validity of this type of assertion are other American businessmen doing business in the country. Expatriate business executives abroad are a tight community with a common interest in sharing information. Foreign chambers of commerce are excellent sources of information (there is usually an American chamber of commerce in each country). In determining whether a particular assertion is correct, bear in mind the possibility of collusion between the foreign company and the foreign government during negotations. Rather than, or in addition to, asking the foreign government what its policy is on an issue under negotiation, you may be able to get a better idea of its actual policies by finding out the terms of other agreements that have received its imprimatur.

Good Cop, Bad Cop

He is alone, yet playing two parts.

—*Korean Proverb*

Present fears are less than horrible imaginings.

—*William Shakespeare,* Macbeth

This form of gamesmanship is known by a number of other names, including "Mutt and Jeff," "tough guy-nice guy," and "fire and water." Whatever the name may be, the approach typically involves at least two individuals on a negotiating team. The first negotiator is notable for her reasonableness and empathy. She may not agree with your position but is inevitably kind and polite and will make an effort to really listen to your concerns. This first negotiator is the "good cop." The other negotiator is notable for her unreasonableness and unprincipled "hard-line" bargaining. This "bad cop" may be prone to unreasonable outbursts and often will make threatening statements. In this scenario, the cops are working together, despite appearances. The good cop will usually contrive or maneuver to create a situation in which the bad cop is not present. During this period, the good cop may acknowledge the legitimacy of your position but will stress the need for concessions on your part to satisfy the bad cop. The good cop acts as a middleman, pushing you to make concessions. Negotiators will often make concessions to the good cop to avoid the worse of the two evils. In some cases, you may never encounter the bad cop because in fact he does not exist. A lawyer will often claim that his unreasonable and irrational client must receive a concession to be satisfied, while in fact the affable client would have happily accepted your first offer.

An example of good cop, bad cop gamesmanship occurred in negotiations between the United States and the People's Republic of China on the Taiwan arms sale issue. Foreign Minister Huang Hua was the rigidly uncompromising bad cop, while Deng Xiaoping played the good cop. It is common in Asian countries for a more junior bureaucrat to play the part of the bad cop. In Western countries the situation is usually reversed. A British mid-level executive will often play off the foil of a senior management "heavy." Combating the good cop, bad cop approach is best accomplished by informing the two cops that you will deal with only one negotiator rather than two. Your goal is to force the two negotiators to reach a common position to which you can respond. Ignore the tactics and instead attack the principles that underlie their demands. As with many of these gamesman's tactics, the good cop, bad cop routine may also be countered successfully by adopting the same approach yourself. You would just love to give the good cop what he wants but you've got a bad cop of your own to placate. If you decide to utilize this approach, it is important that the person playing the heavy not desire to have a continuing relationship with the other negotiator.

Threats

More are threatened than are stabbed.

—*Spanish Proverb*

Philip II, the King of Macedon and the father of Alexander the Great, was able to conquer or form alliances with all of the major Greek city-states except Sparta. When negotiations with the Spartans broke down, Philip sent the following threat by messenger: "You are advised to submit without further delay, for if I bring my army on your land, I will destroy your farms, slay your people, and raze your city." The Spartans sent a one-word reply: "If." Because of Sparta's fierce military reputation, Philip decided discretion was the better part of valor and left the Spartans alone.

The use of threats in a negotiation is one of the oldest and most common forms of gamesmanship. Some threats are made with careful foresight and planning. Others are made impulsively as an emotional reaction. However they are made, threats must take one of two forms: (1) threats that promise retaliation in the event another party takes a certain action or (2) threats that promise punishment if the other party fails to take a certain action. The nature of a threat will also vary depending on whether it is directed at the negotiators or at the organization they represent.

One form of threatening behavior is to make excessive and highly emotional demands on the other negotiator in an attempt to instill fear. After a pause timed to maximize fear, the threatening negotiator then offers to reduce the excessive demands in return for concessions.

Unprincipled negotiators will often attack you rather than your position or the problem. This form of gamesmanship has been utilized by unprincipled negotiators since ancient times. Cicero advised, "When you have no basis for argument, abuse the plaintiff." This negotiating ploy is intended to take advantage of any fear or insecurity on your part. Lower-level American employees and diplomats acting as negotiators are often told by foreigners that they will be punished when their superiors learn of their unwillingness to "cooperate." In most cases, it's just the human equivalent of a false charge in the animal kingdom; a little show of bravado to help establish the hierarchy. By disregarding it as a bit of ritualistic buffoonery, you should be able to secure a credible position for yourself.

Threats are more common in the business community than unseasoned players may expect. An Australian solicitor relays this story about a negotiation he was involved in while working in Hong Kong. The incident arose when he was acting for a Japanese client who was involved in a joint-venture dispute with his coventurer, a Hong Kong Chinese named Wong. The Aussie attorney told us the following story:

> The joint venture had collapsed and we were endeavouring to negotiate a buy-out. After lengthy negotiation I secured what I believed to be a sensational result for the Japanese client and was seeking his final instructions to accept the terms. He told me he required one week to consider the terms.

Two days later I received a call from the solicitor acting for Wong asking whether I knew anything about the mobsters who had confronted his client and threatened to blow his kneecaps off unless he agreed to more stringent terms of settlement with the Japanese coventurer. Of course, I denied any knowledge of this incident and immediately contacted my client. When confronted, he confirmed that he had spoken briefly with his friends at the Yakuza regarding his problems negotiating a settlement and had asked for their assistance in "persuading" his coventurer to accept better terms. Wanting no part in such Wong-doing, I immediately ceased acting for the client.

A friend of the authors was present at a negotiation in which an American threatened the livelihood of a Mexican manufacturer. Among the threats made by the belligerent American was a promise that the Mexican would be "ruined" and "would never work again in the industry." After the American secured his desired concessions and returned to the hotel, he launched into self-congratulatory boasting. The victory was Pyrrhic, however. Word of the American's reputation spread, and it was he rather than the Mexican who was ruined and never worked in the industry again. Other manufacturers simply refused to do business with him. The long-term cost of threats (particularly personal threats) almost always offsets any short-term gain.

While threats can take various forms, your first response to receiving a threat should be to assess its credibility and to determine the consequences of its implementation. The proper response will vary depending upon whether there is any real probability the threat will be carried out or whether any value could be lost. The possible responses to a threat are:

- Challenging the credibility of the threat;
- Challenging that value will be lost if the threat is implemented;
- Intentionally ignoring or "misunderstanding" the threat;
- Implementing the consequences of the threat yourself;
- Counterthreats.

Of all the forms of gamesmanship, the use of counterthreats is the most dangerous as it creates an opportunity for escalation. Multiple counterthreats often escalate out of control. War is a process in which everyone loses. Martin Luther King, Jr., had precisely this in mind when he said, "That old law about 'an eye for an eye' leaves everybody blind." One type of counterthreat that is particularly dangerous is threatening the relationship. As has been emphasized previously, damaging a relationship damages precisely what you need in order to advance the negotiation.

Rather than responding to a threat with a counterthreat, it is preferable that you adopt one of the following tactics:

1. Pause. Request a recess in the negotiation to reassess your position. The passage of time and a new venue alone can dissipate a threat.

2. Challenge the unprincipled nature of the threat. This approach requires that you convince the other negotiator to examine the premises on which a position or demand is based. Be careful that this is not misinterpreted as a counterthreat. The key to making a successful challenge based on principles is to focus on the unconstructive nature of the threat.

3. Sidestep the threat. Often the best approach is to ignore (or pretend to misunderstand the threat) and refocus the discussion on principles and problem solving. Keeping the negotiation moving by asking questions can help you in getting the other negotiator to retreat from his or her threat. In responding to your question, the other negotiator is forced to begin talking again. This may diffuse anger and bring new information into play that can be used to find a creative solution. Also, holding your ground and not being intimidated by the threat lets the other negotiator's ritualistic test of wills play itself out and may allow you to proceed with the negotiations with a more solid relationship established between you.

Bringing Someone Else into the Negotiation

The strong minded is able to hold the fortunes of the enemy in his hands by creating the third element to ensure the desired outcome.

—Sun Tzu

When a foreign business executive does not want to make a concession and has no principled reason for holding out, he or she may decide to bring some other party to the negotiating table who has strong reasons against making the concession. Often, the new party to the negotiation is the foreign government. The response of the foreign negotiators using this form of gamesmanship runs something like, "We would love it, but our hands are tied by the government." Foreign business executives may also bring a domestic special interest group to the table (farmers or students, for example) who oppose the concession. Some negotiators call this tactic the "public propaganda" ploy. Most often, the new person or group is never physically at the negotiation but may be voicing its opposition in the press or directly to the public. Just prior to each round of aviation negotiations between the U.S. and Korean governments in the mid-1980s, representatives of the U.S. airlines involved would await the inevitable editorial on the subject in one of Seoul's major English-language newspapers. Always appearing within a few days of the resumption of negotiations, the editorial would stridently announce the positions to be put forth by the Korean government in the negotiations. The Korean government, in turn, would often refer to these "pressures" as the basis of its positions.

In some cases, the third party may be holding a violent demonstration just outside the negotiating venue. In Mexico, the practice of using the press to place pressure on opposing negotiators has been institutionalized. Payments to reporters to carry specific stories have been given the name "gacetillas." U.S. trade negotiators understand that Mexican politicians who oppose any given proposal will not hesitate to make payments to the press to create negative coverage and scathing editorials.

A friend of the authors' represented a client faced with the nationalization of its lucrative mining operations in Chile during the short tenure of Marxist President Salvador Allende in the early 1970s. The government was offering a pittance as compensation, and negotiations were going nowhere fast. In a final attempt to save the investment, the client decided to bring several other parties to the negotiating table. Ten percent of the operation was quickly sold to a local private company, a Japanese trading company, a German customer of the mine, and a British investment banker. While the shares had to be sold at a substantial discount, four new groups had an immediate stake in the nationalization negotiations. In addition, three foreign governments began to put pressure on the Chilean government not to nationalize the mine.

This form of gamesmanship has been used to achieve noble objectives in some cases. For example, in negotiating with the Marxist government of Ethiopia, a drought relief organization was faced with a seemingly unbreakable barrier when government officials stopped all shipments on the grounds that the food supplied would be used to feed hostile military insurgents. To break the impasse, the relief organization conducted a blitz-krieg, worldwide public relations campaign that effectively brought the governments of other nations to the bargaining table. Through a persistent effort, the relief organization was able to get the Ethiopian government to allow the food shipments to reach the drought victims.

Stressful Environment and Entrapment

The most valuable system is a good nervous system.

—*B. C. Forbes*

If you can't stand the heat, get out of the kitchen.

—*Harry S Truman*

Illegitimi non carborundum (Don't let the bastards grind you down).

—*Roman Proverb*

Stress is the nonspecific response of the body to demands placed upon it. Virtually every aspect of life produces stress.

A graphic representation of the relationship between stress and negotiating performance would take the form of a bell curve. An absence of any form of stress produces no performance since this state is achievable only in death. As the level of stress rises from low to moderate, performance will improve. Eventually, increases in the level of stress will produce a "breaking point," after which performance will deteriorate (in many cases radically). This breaking point varies from individual to individual. Each of us needs to find our limitations and construct defenses that keep us from passing into the danger zone of deteriorating performance. What each of us must find is the right level of stress. Foreign negotiators have been known to seek advantage in a negotation by creating an environment that is overly stressful to the American negotiators.

An unprincipled negotiator can create excessive levels of stress in many ways, such as creating a deadline for agreement or making threats. Personal antagonism on the part of other negotiators can also create stress. Another example of stress adversely affecting a person's negotiating skills occurs when air-conditioning is not provided to the negotiation venue in extremely hot weather. Similarly, heat may not be provided in extremely cold weather. One of the authors learned quickly when negotiating in Beijing in the winter to always don long underwear and to bring a hat and gloves. In these instances, the lack of heat in the buildings was probably not a negotiating ploy on the part of the Chinese. Nonetheless, it certainly constitutes a significant disadvantage for an unprepared American negotiator.

Stress can also be created by exposing the Americans to hostile third parties or by creating inordinate delays in the negotiating process. The 1972 Nixon-Brezhnev Moscow summit is a good example of negotiators attempting to utilize a stressful environment to produce concessions by the other side. The Soviet negotiators frequently changed the setting and agenda of meetings and refused to provide the Americans with the usual access to telecommunication facilities as well as administrative and logistical support. Justified fears by U.S. negotiators that the Soviets were electronically monitoring their conversations added to the stress.

Belligerent and other aggressive forms of behavior by the other negotiators can also create a stressful environment. Sir Rudolf Bing, the famous general manager of the Metropolitan Opera, encountered this form of gamesmanship during negotiations with the union representing the stagehands. After being verbally assaulted during one particularly hostile negotiating session with the union, Bing leaned across the table toward the trade union's lawyer and said, "I'm awfully sorry, I didn't get that. Would you mind screaming it again?"

A person's ability to function effectively in a negotiation may also be undermined by entrapment. Probably the most common form of entrapment is the emotional investment we make in the negotiation process itself. Too many American business executives, once having made a decision to do business in a foreign country or with a foreign company, are so anxious to conclude a deal that they do so for the wrong reasons. Again and again, American business executives travel to foreign countries and feel they have failed unless they return to the United States with a contract in hand after the first or second visit. This feeling is reinforced by the substantial expenses incurred while they are investigating deals and negotiating in the foreign country. Not doing business in a particular country or with a particular company may be the best available alternative in a given negotiation. You should always keep in mind that amounts already invested and effort already expended are irrelevant to a wise decision maker. As the dismal scientists are wont to say: Sunk costs are irrelevant. It is hard to walk away from a deal that you have worked hard to implement for months and even years. However, the deal itself is not the objective. If the deal can't justify itself going forward, the best alternative to a negotiated agreement is to walk away, no matter how great your disappointment.

Entrapment can also occur when anger at past and current events leads to a desire on your part to punish the other side. In retrospect, even successful efforts to achieve vengeance are usually unsatisfactory and unworthy of the effort involved. Moving on to new challenges is likely to be more productive than efforts at seeking retribution. Of course, there is a subtle yet important difference between seeking retribution and establishing a reputation for protecting your interests. The former action is a waste of time, while the latter can be essential.

Another cause of entrapment can be a person's pride. We have an acquaintance in Australia who owns a company that extracts and delivers iron ore to bulk carriers for shipment to Europe and Japan. He tells the story of two shipping magnates who were involved in a fierce battle to capture the lion's share of the iron ore bulk-carrier business between Australia and Europe (presumably the lion was out of the picture at this point). One shipping magnate was Greek and the other Norwegian. The Norwegian was more established and could offer more regular service, so the Greek cut his prices by ten percent. The Norwegian responded by cutting his prices an additional ten percent. The Greek was furious and cut his prices by another ten percent. The Norwegian cut his prices again by the same amount. Clearly, the men were locked in a test of wills and had long since abandoned rational pricing strategies. The Norwegian shipping magnate finally held the line on prices and allowed the Greek to undercut him by ten percent. The share of Australia's iron ore moving on the Greek's carriers soared. This situation continued for six months. What the Greek magnate did not realize was that the Norwegian was buying large amounts of iron ore in Australia and shipping it to Europe at a huge profit. The Norwegian made a rational decision that he could make more money by shipping iron ore on the Greek's ships than by cutting prices. The Greek had let his pride interfere with good business.

Guilt

It is a great comfort to be free of guilt.

—Cicero

Sacrifice is a form of bargaining.

—Holbrook Jackson

Because the United States is viewed as a strong economic power, foreign negotiators will often try to evoke your sympathy by proclaiming their relative poverty, inexperience, and weakness. Typically, the foreign negotiator using this approach will not contest the reasonableness of your position and will instead focus on his needs. Responses such as "I agree with you, but we need this" are common. During a bilateral trade negotiation between Korea and the United States, a senior Korean negotiator explained that he fully agreed with the rationale behind the position of the Americans. However, he said the concession asked for by the Koreans was like a small strawberry that had fallen off a huge and elaborate banquet table that was America's sole domain. The Korean asked with indignance how a country with so much could deprive a hungry orphan from a small morsel of food. To counter this form of gamesmanship, force the other negotiators to explain the principles behind their position. Until you have examined the other side's principles, you have nothing to challenge.

Foreign negotiators may try to make you feel guilty in order to make you susceptible to giving concessions. The most important rule to remember in this situation is that there is never a need to accept guilt that has not been earned. If you refuse to accept unearned guilt, the other negotiators may attempt to ascribe guilt to you for some transgression that is your fault. You may be late for a meeting or unable to produce a document in time. If they try to make you feel guilty, apologize if you must, but do not let them manipulate your behavior. A humorous example involving the use of guilt in international negotiations involved opera star Birgit Marta Nilsson. On one occasion she was negotiating a contract with Herbert von Karajan, at the time director of the Vienna Opera, when a string of pearls she was wearing broke and scattered all over the floor. Von Karajan and several others who were present got down on their knees to search for the pearls. "We must find every one of them," von Karajan said. "These are the expensive pearls that Miss Nilsson buys with her high fees from the Metropolitan." "No," Miss Nilsson replied, "these are just imitation ones, which I buy with my low fees from the Vienna Opera."

Patterned Concessions

A wise man can achieve his objective by openly disclosing what is false and hiding what is true ("Deceive the Sky and Cross the Ocean").

—*Chinese Proverb*

A skillful negotiator can often create a false impression regarding his acceptable settlement range by making patterned concessions. The best way to explain this form of gamesmanship is through an example. In one case, an African government offered to pay $10 million as compensation for a nationalized factory of a U.S. company. The next offer of settlement from the African government was $15 million and the following offer $17.5 million. By patterning its concessions, the African government had subtly begun to convey a message that it would be willing to settle the matter for between $18 million and $20 million. In fact, the Africans were willing to go as high as $30 million to avoid scaring off other foreign investors. By creating the artificial pattern, the U.S. company was given the false impression that a settlement of more than $20 million was not possible.

The French novelist Honoré de Balzac used a variation of the patterned-concession strategy to purchase a vase with an asking price that was beyond his means. Repeated attempts by Balzac to bargain down the price of the vase were unsuccessful. Balzac did not give up and enlisted three of his friends in a carefully scripted plan. The first friend entered the shop and made an offer, lower than the marked price. The next day, the second friend made a bid which was lower than the first. On the next day, the third bidder made a strong effort to get it at his ridiculously low figure. Balzac returned and offered more than the last three bids. The plan worked and Balzac got the vase at his price.

Differentiating between a false pattern and a real indication of an acceptable settlement range is never easy. While there is no secret method for discovering a false concession pattern, closely examining the reasons behind an offer, and not the offer itself, can provide you with excellent clues.

CEREMONY

Ceremony keeps up all things. 'Tis like a penny glass to a rich spirit, or some excellent water. Without it, the water were spilt, the spirit lost.

—*John Selden*

Men are never more offended than when we depreciate their ceremonies and usages. Seek to oppress them, and it is sometimes a proof of the esteem with which you regard them; depreciate their customs, it is always the mark of contempt.

—*Baron de Montesquieu*

Ceremony is the smoke of friendship.

—*Chinese Proverb*

Lao Tzu wrote in the fifth century B.C. that "ceremonies are the outward expression of inner feeling." The sage's words are no less true in contemporary society. Many American business executives believe that the ceremonies that are part of the negotiation process are time-consuming, useless, and an unnecessary expense. This attitude reflects the relative unimportance of ceremony in modern American life generally. This arises, in part, because the United States as a culture is still young, and it reflects the future orientation of youth. In part, it reflects the lack of a common past of a nation of immigrants. Most other cultures ascribe far more importance to ceremonies, and abiding by them can be helpful in making the nature of your actions and promises meaningful to the negotiator of the other culture.

The lack of ceremony in American culture is only relative. Americans, like all humans, have a need for tangible manifestations of what we believe. Many psychologists, most notably Carl Jung, believe that man's ability to manipulate symbols is what distinguishes the species. Ceremonies can tie you to your past, invest you with authority, and link you with your spiritual beliefs. One of the world's most innovative and successful educators, the famous educator Maria Montessori, performed extensive research in Holland and learned that people understand images more easily than words and that showing is more effective than telling. These discoveries are extensively used in the network of schools that bear her name. You can use ceremonies as a method of communicating your good intentions, as well as your aspirations for the business collaboration.

Ceremonies provide each party to a negotiation with tangible representations of complex and uncertain abstractions. Ceremonies do not need to be ancient or venerable to be effective. The ceremony focuses the awareness of the participants on some form of transition to a new or different relationship. While ceremonies can cost money and delay, the benefits can far outweigh the costs.

Some cultures will go to extraordinary expense to satisfy what they believe to be ceremonial requirements of other cultures. A friend of ours who was one of the small number of American lawyers admitted to practice law in Japan after the Second World War was retained by a Japanese client to represent it in one of the first Eurobond offerings by a Japanese company. The British investment bank Rothschilds, acting as the underwriter, informed the Japanese that its solicitor would be present during the negotiations in London. Our friend was flown to London from Tokyo and was involved in the first day's negotiations. The Japanese were informed at the end of the day that the British solicitor could not be present the next day because of a conflict. The American lawyer was instructed by his Japanese client not to attend the next day's meeting. The British solicitor's conflict continued to occupy him, and the American lawyer proceeded to spend two lovely weeks in London in the spring awaiting instructions to reenter the negotiations. As long as the solicitor was absent, the ceremonial need on the part of the Japanese to have their counterpart in attendance was also absent.

Depending on the culture of the other negotiator, some form of ceremony should be held to memorialize the result of the negotiation. The nature of the ceremonial stage will vary widely depending upon the particular culture with which you are dealing. The most common ceremony is the banquet or party that accompanies the execution of an agreement or the beginning of a relationship. In some cultures, the ceremony may verge on what you would consider the ridiculous. In Asia you may need to hire a geomancer to conduct a *feng shui* ceremony before breaking ground on the construction of a hotel. In some Third-World countries you may need to hire a shaman to bless the project. Even if a ritual or ceremony may seem strange, failure to participate can convey a lack of commitment to the venture. It may be necessary for the chairman or president of your company to make a special overseas trip just for the purpose of the ceremony. Generally, a ceremony marks a transition rather than the end of a negotiation.

One footnote with regard to ceremonies in international negotiations is worthy of note. Americans, particularly lawyers, like to call the signing of a contract for a major transaction a "closing." This term clearly conveys the attitude that the placing of pen on paper ends the negotiation process. This is precisely the attitude that one must avoid in an international setting. Negotiation is better viewed as a dialectical process without a beginning, a middle, or an end. The signing of a contract or an exchange of documents should be associated with the beginning, enlargement, or enhancement of a relationship. To be sure, some contracts do mark the closing of a relationship (such as a settlement with a bankrupt debtor), but this is not necessarily the case.

IMPLEMENTATION AND DYNAMIC RENEGOTIATION

One of the most publicized joint ventures between a U.S. company and the People's Republic of China occurred as a result of a 1980 visit to Beijing by Armand Hammer, the chairman of Occidental Petroleum. Hammer was experienced in dealing with Communist regimes since he had done business with every Soviet leader from Stalin to Brezhnev. After investigating a number of potential projects in the PRC, Hammer decided to enter into a joint venture to build an enormous open-pit coal mine. Although negotiations regarding the project began immediately, an agreement still had not been reached a year later. The lack of progress occurred despite the opening of a Beijing office by the subsidiary of Occidental Petroleum (Island Creek Coal Company) and repeated visits by Chinese delegations to Occidental's facilities in the United States and three visits by Hammer himself to the PRC.

Contrary to numerous optimistic reports issued by Hammer's public relations staff, the two sides were locked in acrimonious arguments about costs, assumption of risk, who had greater expertise, and the proper division of profits. Both Occidental and the Chinese came close to claiming the other side was dishonest and dealing in bad faith. Despite the serious nature of the disputes, Hammer skillfully kept the disputes from the public. He knew that if the press were to learn about the problems and make them public, the desire of both sides to "save face" could prevent agreement.

The negotiations between Occidental and the PRC continued for over five years before producing an agreement. Of course, the negotiations between the PRC and Occidental continue even today. At every turn, the PRC is pushing to increase its return by inflating the costs of goods and services that it provides to the joint venture.

The Chinese have a saying, "He ging, he li, he fa," which defies precise translation but which can be said to mean: "In resolving disputes, first examine the relationship between the parties, then consider right and wrong, and only then pay attention to the law." There is considerable wisdom in adopting this approach. Americans too often bring a "deal" mentality to negotiations. If a problem exists, the American mentality is, "Let's sit down and thrash this thing out." Linear problem-solving skills are then used to make a deal. The agreement memorializing the deal marks the end of the problem and is expected to make the deal self-implementing and self-policing. This deal mentality is essentially static in orientation, while the world actually exists in a dynamic state. As time passes, the deal and the contract memorializing it increasingly cease to reflect the realities of a dynamic relationship. Renegotiation thus is required.

The evolution from rural village life to modern urban society has been accompanied by a breakdown of the social support of relationships and informal sanctions for their breach. Particularly in the post–World War II era, the role of social structures such as family, community, and religion in enforcing obligations has given way to more formal legalistic mechanisms. Our mobile, urban culture increasingly relies on legal relationships to enforce obligations. The legal system upon which we are placing greater reliance, however, has become no less unwieldy. A solid relationship is clearly a more effective policing mechanism than an "airtight" contract, particularly when dealing across cultures with multiple legal and governmental jurisdictions. The goal of the global negotiator should be to develop mutually dependent strategic relationships that recreate within the global village the mutual support structures of our long-lost village ancestors.

In international negotiations, the challenge of "staying at yes" is no less difficult than "getting to yes." While both domestic and international business relationships require continual renegotiation to remain fruitful, there are special factors in the international context that heighten the amount of renegotiation required. First, the risk of change is typically greater in an international negotiation. When more than one country is involved, negotiators must deal with changes such as wars, revolutions, coups, trade embargoes, currency devaluations, and changes in government policies. Events like the U.S. invasion of Panama by President Bush, the fall of the Shah of

Iran, the departure of Ferdinand Marcos from the Philippines, or the closing of the Suez Canal due to Israeli hostilities do not affect a deal to sell Washington state apples in California, but they do create a need to renegotiate many types of international relationships. Second, many cultures simply do not view a signed contract as an exclusive definition of the deal. These cultures reject the notion that "a deal is a deal." Instead, many other cultures view the deal as being the relationship between the parties. This relationship must evolve, like all healthy relationships, and this evolution requires constant renegotiation.

During the implementation stage of an international negotiation, dynamic renegotiation will occur on a continual basis. This renegotiation is no less important than the primary negotiation. The same negotiation skills and effort are necessary for success in the renegotiations. Only by continuing to negotiate well can the negotiations sustain the positive result of the initial negotiation.

Manage Conflict

Keep Public Disputes Private

> But it is at home and not in public that one should wash one's dirty linen.
>
> —Napoleon Bonaparte

> . . . it takes only common sense derived from daily experience to realize that it is impossible to negotiate in public on anything in which parties other than the negotiators are interested.
>
> —H. J. Morgenthau

> . . . the day on which there will be no secret negotiations, there will be no negotiations.
>
> —Jules Cambon

When details of a negotiation become known to the public, negotiators are likely to consider not only how their interests are served by a proposed agreement but how the agreement will affect other interested individuals and groups. Worse, the negotiators may "play" to an outside audience in order to satisfy their own egos rather than the interests of those whom they represent. When particularly important negotiations are taking place in full public view, a type of "Super Bowl" mentality can arise wherein each party is afraid to take risks or consider new ideas for fear of looking foolish. Sports commentators have noted how, since that great media event was conceived, the teams tend to play extremely conservatively in the Super Bowl. The result of this conservatism more often than not is a boring football game. (The commercials, on the other hand, get better every year.) The result of audience-imposed conservatism in a negotiation is worse. Negotiators who are afraid to take risks or consider new approaches because of concerns about how the public will respond will have difficulty creating new value. The resulting competitive, rather than collaborative, struggle will tend to produce a less than optimum result.

One hallmark of U.S.-Soviet negotiations has been the inability of the United States to keep proceedings secret. The leaks to the press that plague the U.S. government at all levels do much to damage the relationship between the two nations. Creativity and brainstorming are not possible in an environment subject to public scrutiny. This is why some of the best and most creative negotiating is done in places like the cloakroom of the Untied States Senate, which the press, public, and lobbyists are not allowed to enter.

Many experienced negotiators make it their first order of business to reach agreement with the other side on a publicity blackout during the entire course of the negotiations. Under this approach, all negotiators are barred from making statements to the press until an agreement is reached. This approach was used with great success in the Camp David negotiations between Israel and Egypt. Keeping the negotiation *process* secret is not sinister as long as the *outcome* is made public. A prominent scholar of diplomacy has called for "open covenants—but unopenly arrived at" as a remedy for the Super Bowl psychology plaguing international negotiations.

Former Ambassador John W. McDonald tells the following story about the value of secrecy in international negotiations:

In 1979 I was involved in a conference to negotiate a treaty against the taking of hostages. This, of course, was a very delicate thing with Libya and Syria and the Soviet Union. Thirty-six countries were involved in the process. They met for three years, three weeks at a time, with no success whatsoever.

Before the last meeting, we looked at the model of what had happened before and why it had failed. We felt that it had failed because the previous sessions were public and on the record. In other words, every speaker was simply talking to his home audience, making the points that the foreign office had said he should be making. Nothing was happening. We were trying to develop a treaty which would fill a legal hole so that a hostage-taker had to be either extradited for prosecution or prosecuted where he was arrested.

We tried something different in the third and probably final three-week session. After the opening morning we proposed that this same group of thirty-six nations turn itself into an informal working group not open to the public. That meant no records of any kind, no secretariat, no press, and therefore, in practice, no speeches since no one was there to listen.

The delegates immediately got down to work and we negotiated and interacted informally, ten to twelve hours a day. The last day of the three-week session we reconvened in plenary session, open to the public, and adopted a draft treaty. I am convinced that the conference model made the difference.

Two factors have made it increasingly difficult for international negotiators to work effectively in view of the public. First, the electronic media, instantaneous communication, and jet travel have made it much easier for information to be disseminated to the public. An Australian in an outback sheep station can learn about a development in negotiations between his govenment and Japan minutes after it happens. He and his drinking buddies can react immediately to create political pressure constraining the Australian negotiator. (In other words, it's not so easy to pull the wool over their eyes.) The second development limiting the effectiveness of negotiators operating in public view has been the increase in the number and political power of special-interest groups during the 1970s and 1980s. Some group can be found that opposes nearly anything, with the result being negotiation gridlock.

Resolve Disputes Quickly and Simply

Americans are typically quick to turn to formal legal processes to resolve a dispute. Litigation should be considered a last-resort alternative when you are doing business internationally. Business executives from other cultures are more accustomed than Americans to working out disputes privately. Furthermore, once litigation has started, "honor" or "face" may preclude doing business during the lawsuit (or anytime in the future). Americans, who generally feel less constrained by these considerations, may think nothing of doing business with a company with which they are engaged in a bitter court battle. Few foreign companies feel the same way. For many foreign business executives, litigation requires a complete severing of all business ties.

The simplest way to resolve conflicts is to anticipate them and to act quickly and constructively when they arise. A number of airlines have adopted a policy of providing extraordinary immediate assistance to friends and relatives of victims of airplane crashes. These airlines spare no expense in flying bereaved families to the crash site, retrieving personal effects from the wreckage, flying the injured passengers to the finest hospitals, and providing psychological assistance. Experience shows that fewer legal actions are filed when an airline reacts constructively by conducting an immediate victim-and-relative-assistance blitzkrieg, rather than reacting defensively in anticipation of litigation. Whatever the motivation, few would disagree with the appropriateness of the airlines' response.

Americans are not the only nationality that can be overly rights-conscious and legalistic. An issue arose early in a negotiation between an eminent solicitor from London representing a large British bank, and the Polish government, concerning the ability of the British bank to seize vessels that were docked in ports in Western nations in order to pay debts owed by the Polish government. When the issue was raised, the solicitor began a long soliloquy in which he described the procedure for arresting a vessel in a foreign port, selling the vessel at auction, and then using the money raised to pay off the debt. The solicitor named several relevant international conventions, cited numerous important cases, and quoted from leading legal commentators. When the solicitor finished his long-winded oration, he smiled confidently. The chief Polish negotiator barked, "So what?" The British solicitor stammered, "You will need to do better than that in court!" The Polish negotiator replied without expression, "We are not in court. We are negotiating. Let's negotiate." The solicitor was never quite the same after this early deflation and achieved a meager result for his client.

Because Americans have traditionally relied on courts and other formal legal mechanisms for resolving disputes, the term *alternative dispute resolution* (ADR) has been coined to encompass all alternatives. ADR methods include mediation, fact finders without authority, arbitration, and summary trials. It may or may not be an indication of the ascendancy of ADR methods that in a recent poll more Americans were able to identify Judge Wapner of television's "People's Court" than Chief Justice Rehnquist of the U.S. Supreme Court. (Harvard Law Professor Alan Dershowitz, on the other hand, has opined that the greater recognition of the former properly reflects the relative abilities of the two jurists.)

The number of "alternative" ways of resolving a dispute is limited only by your imagination. One relatively simple technique involves bringing in executives from both companies who have no prior involvement in the dispute. Often the fresh perspective of these executives serves to facilitate a mutually acceptable solution. The newly involved executives have no entrenched position to defend and can concentrate on finding a resolution to the dispute that benefits both parties.

Mediation is another method that can be used to facilitate the settlement of a dispute. The mediation process involves an impartial third party to assist in reaching an agreement. Utilizing mediation is voluntary and is based on the self-interest of the parties involved. The mediator will, if she is effective, establish a climate free of unproductive emotion and distrust, allowing the parties to communicate more effectively about their differences. A qualified mediator will work to find a solution that satisfies the interests of both parties rather than identifying the positions of the parties and trying to extract concessions. The best mediators are able to divide the orange in such a way that each negotiator feels he received the largest share. Mediation is hard and time-consuming work. As the Japanese say, "The go-between wears a thousand sandals."

One successful mediation effort resulted in the Camp David Accords of 1978, employing what became known as the "one-text" approach. The United States, led by President Jimmy Carter, mediated negotiations between Israel and Egypt at Camp David, Maryland. The U.S. approach involved meeting separately with representatives of the two countries and getting their comments and criticisms on a common working document. Critical to the success of this method was the fact that neither side was pressed to accept or reject the text. Rather, they were asked to help improve upon it before the next revision. When, after 23 rounds of comments and revisions over 13 days, the potential for further improvement was exhausted, only then were Israel and Egypt presented with the text for agreement.

Much of the success of the Camp David negotiations can be credited to the choice of mediators. In contrast, when members of the Reagan administration wanted to begin negotiations with the regime of Ayatollah Khomeini, they chose an Iranian arms dealer named Manucher Ghorbanifar. This choice proved to be inauspicious and resulted in the Iran-Contra arms scandal. A comparison of the Camp David negotiations and Iran-Contra deal shows clearly the correlation between the quality of the mediator and the quality of the mediation.

It is important that the mediation remain a private matter. Once a foreign business executive has adopted a position that is known to the public, it will be difficult to convince him to back down. The conciliation procedure should be simple and a fixed time limit established. Both parties should submit written descriptions of their position, together with copies of all relevant documents, without applying rules of evidence or procedure. Copies of the written submission to the mediator should also be given to the other party. In practice, the result will often be a less than perfect solution, but it may be the only solution that allows the parties to continue doing business.

Don't Burn Bridges

If a decision is made to terminate negotiations, as much care should be taken in doing so as in any other stage of the negotiation. A poorly executed termination can make doing business with the same company in the future impossible, or at least very difficult. You never know when and under what circumstances you may encounter an old sparring partner again. An American pharmaceutical manufacturer, for which one of the author's friends had performed consulting services, was interested in acquiring North American rights to patented technology developed by a German drug company. The Germans were ambivalent about the U.S. market. Profits would be significant once a distribution system was established, but costs would be high, particularly in early years. The U.S. company sent a senior vice-president to Germany to secure the necessary patent licenses. The negotiations went on for several days with little progress. During a particularly tense meeting the American negotiator stated that his company was prepared to pay $1.5 million for the North American rights to the German technology. The managing director of the German pharmaceutical house refused, protesting that the offer did not nearly reflect the value of the patent rights. The American countered, "Will you accept $1.75 million? We can have the money in your hands tomorrow." The Germans dismissed the offer and rose from their chairs as if to leave. The American also rose and said, "O.K., this is my final offer. Three million dollars payable immediately." The Germans sat down and consulted among themselves in their native tongue. "Done," said the German managing director. Several days later, after the lawyers had done their bit, the patent license was signed and the funds were transferred to the Germans. Immediately after the closing ceremony, the American negotiator pulled his German counterpart aside and showed him a certified check for $5 million made out to the German company. "You could have had this if you held out longer," the American said with a chuckle. The German did not find this development amusing. Five years later the American company was in severe financial difficulty. As difficulty became crisis, the German pharmaceutical house stepped in and infused new capital into the American company in return for a majority stock interest. Not long thereafter, a certain senior vice-president was unemployed.

Try to avoid fixing blame, and avoid characterizing the proceedings as a failure. Strive to keep the reasons for any breakdown of negotiations secret from the public, to prevent a loss of face for either party. If possible, try to characterize the situation as a temporary cessation rather than a final and complete termination of the relationship.

Consult before Taking Action

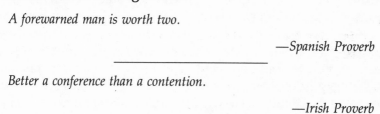

A forewarned man is worth two.

—Spanish Proverb

Better a conference than a contention.

—Irish Proverb

In their book, *Getting Together: Building a Relationship That Gets to Yes*, Roger Fisher and Scott Brown utilize the phrase "always consult before deciding" (ACBD) to describe an important method of improving both a relationship and the result of the negotiation. By consulting with the foreign negotiator, you can achieve a number of objectives. First, you can increase the level of trust since you have shown your concern for how actions may affect the other negotiator. Second, you can discover alternatives that you may never have considered. These alternatives allow you to create new value in the negotiation. Finally, you can avoid unnecessarily damaging the pride or face of the other negotiator. If the other negotiator is not informed of your plans before you take action, he or she will not be able to prepare his or her company or its constituents (shareholders, government officials, and citizens) for the action. This may reduce the negotiator's range of options and produce adverse consequences for one or both of you.

Introducing a possibly controversial proposal during a negotiating session without prior warning can also be risky. A negotiator who is surprised by a proposal can react emotionally in a manner that damages or destroys the ability of the parties to reach an agreement. A better way of presenting a new proposal is to inform the other negotiator about the proposal before a face-to-face meeting. In some cases, it will be useful to transmit the information through a third party. This can allow you to determine the other negotiator's reaction to your proposal with considerably less risk. This prerelease of information or proposals is known as a "trial balloon."

Foreign negotiators will often make proposals that they claim are suggestions made by other parties. For example, the foreign negotiators may say during a negotiation that their legal department or accounting department suggested a particular proposal. Proposals may also be relayed informally between negotiating sessions. For example, it is common for Americans doing business in China to receive a new idea for consideration during a visit to the Great Wall or some other tourist attraction. These suggestions are often intended to be trial balloons that can be quickly withdrawn by the foreign negotiators without a loss of face if you do not respond favorably. Trial balloons can be an effective form of consulting. If no objection is raised to the trial balloon, the proposal can become part of the agreement with little cost. You should deflate any objectionable trial balloons as soon as possible so they do not become a part of the negotiating agenda.

Trial balloons may also be sent up by a foreign government. A classic negotiating tactic used by politicians and bureaucrats is to leak a controversial proposal to the press. The government will then closely watch the trial balloon to see if it is attacked by the public. If the attack by the public is strong, the government can claim the proposal was never seriously considered. If the attack is only moderate, the government can wait and introduce the proposal when the public has become bored with the matter. If opposition is weak or nonexistent, the proposal can be launched immediately. Foreign governments often launch trial balloons in the form of press leaks when negotiating with American companies over market entry.

Experienced negotiators know better than to force their counterparts into a corner from which they cannot escape. Any hope of obtaining the cooperation of a negotiator in such a position in creating a gain is lost. Instead, the cornered negotiator will be preoccupied with reversing the situation. The negotiation inevitably becomes an adversarial contest of resources, stamina, and conviction intended to capture the largest possible portion of a fixed pie. Mutual, collaborative problem solving is seldom the concern of a negotiator who feels threatened. Sun Tzu recognized this fact when he wrote in *The Art of War:*

> When you surround an army, leave an outlet free. This does not mean that the enemy is to be allowed to escape. The object is to make him believe that there is a road to safety, and thus prevent his fighting with the courage of despair. For you should not press a desperate foe too hard.

The other negotiator should always be offered a graceful way out of a predicament. Typically, rather than suggesting a way out of the other negotiator's "box," you should simply recognize the problem and express a willingness to be patient.

Keep the Relationship Mutually Beneficial

Mutual content is like a river, which must have its banks on either side.

—Alain Lesage

Treaties which are not built on reciprocal benefits are not likely to be of long duration.

—George Washington

Identity of interests is the surest of bonds, whether between states or individuals.

—Thucydides

Agreements that are produced by reconciling interests have as their base the mutual satisfaction of all parties. This satisfaction benefits the relationship, which in turn makes disputes less likely to occur. In contrast, agreements that are the result of a power struggle are unlikely to be mutually satisfactory. A structure that is unsatisfactory to any negotiator is unlikely to last and is likely to produce additional disputes. The challenge of an international negotiator is to advance interests while pre-serving the stability of the relationship that is the source of value. Balancing these objects requires judgment and experi-ence. It might (or might not) be helpful to recall the old stock-market adage that "one can make money being a bull or a bear, but not a pig."

Preserving the negotiated agreement can be accomplished by structuring the exchange of commitments properly, as well as by working hard at postnegotiation relations. One way of as-suring that mutual interest continues is to create a commitment to the relationship itself. A negotiator who has invested sig-nificantly in building a relationship will be hesitant to breach an agreement. An investment in the relationship can be created by involving each person in the negotiating process and cre-ating a sense of shared pride.

Sharing value is critical to maintaining a relationship. Smart negotiators learn to share value even when nothing compels them to do so. On a trip to Asia, Georges Clemenceau, the prime minister of France, discovered an antique he desired badly. The dealer said he could have it for only seventy-five rupees, "Because of who you are." Clemenceau offered forty-five rupees. The bargaining went on, with Clemenceau firmly sticking to his forty-five-rupee offer. Eventually, the dealer raised his hands indignantly. "Impossible! I'd rather give it to you!" he exclaimed. "Bon!" agreed Clemenceau, pocketing the antique. "You are exceptionally kind and I thank you, but such a gift could only come from a friend. I hope you will not be insulted if I offer you a gift in return." The dealer politely refused. "Here," said Clemenceau, "are forty-five rupees for you to use in charitable works." The dealer accepted the money, and the men parted on excellent terms.

The apparel company Liz Claiborne is an example of a com-pany that has been able to create strong relationships that survive changing market conditions by dealing with its man-ufacturers as strategic partners. Rather than rushing to a rival manufacturer if it is possible to cut a dollar off the price of a sweater, Liz Claiborne works with its regular sweater manufacturer to achieve the price point for each sweater. The relationship works because each party needs the other. Liz Claiborne needs a good manufacturer, and the manufacturer needs a market for its sweaters. Both benefit from continuity in the relationship. In contrast to this strategic partnership are relationships that are structured with only a discrete transaction in mind.

Granting a professional athlete a guaranteed contract is an example of an arrangement that can undermine mutual interest by breaking the link between the reward received by one party and the overall success of the relationship. Many sports franchise owners have come to regret guaranteeing the salary of a sports star without including performance incentives in the contract. A lack of mutual interest, even if it results from an arrangement strongly favored by one of the parties, can damage the relationship to the detriment of both parties.

Benjamin Franklin, a renowned diplomat, among other occupations and avocations, recognized the value of creating mutual interest when he wrote:

> Trades would not take place unless it were advantageous to the parties concerned. Of course, it is better to strike as good a bargain as one's bargaining position admits. The worst outcome is when by overriding greed, no bargain is struck, and a trade that could have been advantageous to both parties, does not come off at all.

One useful approach to keeping an international contract mutually beneficial is to allocate the respective risks of the relationship to the party who has the ability to control or affect the risk. In a contract with the Argentine government, it would serve the relationship to have the risk of a devaluation in the Argentine currency rest with that government. In return, you could agree to be responsible for increases in shipping charges.

There is nothing as inevitable in life as change. What may seem fixed in concrete today is dust in the wind tomorrow. In 1943 IBM Chairman Thomas Watson wrote: "I think there's a world market for about five computers." In 1946 Darryl Zanuck commented on television by saying that "people will soon get tired of staring at the plywood box every night." Because situations inevitably change, so will the interests of parties to an agreement. As these interests evolve, so must the relationship if it is to remain mutually beneficial. Obsolete agreements tend to be breached, and one-sided relationships aren't durable.

A good example of a conflict that resulted from a failure to maintain mutual interest in a relationship began with negotiations between Australian and Japanese companies in the 1970s. The Japanese companies recognized the need for more iron ore and coal for Japan's thriving industries. They also knew that Australia had these resources. However, huge investments would be needed to bring the resources from the mines to Japan's bulk carriers. The Japanese offered to invest in joint ventures that would own and develop the resources. The Australians were extremely leery about the Japanese ownership of resources within their borders so they decided to borrow huge amounts in international financial markets to build the necessary infrastructure themselves. The Japanese and the Australians then entered into contracts providing for the sale of the coal and iron ore at specific prices per metric ton. Most of these contracts did not contain "take-or-pay" provisions requiring the Japanese firms to pay even if they did not take delivery of the coal and iron ore. By the time the necessary infrastructure was built and the resources were ready to bring to market, the world price of coal and iron ore was above the agreed price and the relationship worked well. The Australians sold their entire output and used part of the proceeds to meet their debt servicing obligations. The rest was profit. Trouble began, however, when the price of the resources fell to well below the agreed price per ton. The Japanese companies then repudiated the contracts and refused to take delivery of the coal and iron ore. The Japanese suggested new contracts at lower prices. The Australians protested strenuously but received only statements from the Japanese stressing the need to keep the relationship mutually beneficial. The Australians refused and threatened legal action. In response, the Japanese companies stopped sending ships to Australia and instead sent them to load coal and iron ore in Canada, the United States, and Brazil. Faced with default on the loans used to finance the coal and iron ore infrastructure, the Australians were forced to capitulate and agree to sell to the Japanese at the lower price.

How could this situation have been avoided by the Australians? The deal between the Australian and Japanese companies should have been structured so that the Japanese also had an interest in getting the coal and iron ore to market at the best possible price. One way of accomplishing this would have been to allow the Japanese firms to purchase an interest in the mines and infrastructure so there would be a mutual interest in maintaining a good price for the resources. Another approach would have been for the Australians to have borrowed the funds from Japan instead of from the Euromarkets. The prospect of a default on the debt would have made it difficult for the Japanese to stop sending their ships to Australia.

The key to long-term viability is to keep the relationship mutually beneficial. In most instances, this means being both a student and a teacher in a business relationship. In selecting business partners, Asians have been guided by teachings exemplified by the statement made by a Zen master named Zhantang:

> When you seek an associate, it should be one who is worthy of being your teacher, one whom you will always honor and respect, and one you can take for an example in doing things, so there will be some benefit in your association. You should still follow a teacher who is just a little better than you, to be alerted to what you have not reached.

Entering into any form of business collaboration without a desire to learn from your partner is rarely a beneficial arrangement in the long term.

This book has repeatedly made the point that doing business overseas is a long-term undertaking. Companies that base their decisions on maximizing short-term gain seldom persevere in the world of international business. Those American companies that are successful in the long run realize that a stable and prosperous business relationship requires that both companies continue to realize meaningful value as long as the relationship continues.

Another major theme of this book is that a static, deal orientation to negotiation is ill-suited to a rapidly changing global environment. A negotiated agreement can't comprehend all the changing circumstances to which the relationship will be subjected. To create durable relationships, focus on the interests of both parties and remain aware that those interests too will change. Awareness of the negotiation process itself is essential if cultural assumptions are not to blind you to the realities of the interaction. Ethnocentrism can obscure our view of even the most obvious opportunities; judgment constrains our vision. The global perspective comprehends the whole and looks toward the future.

4

Conclusion (and Beginning)

What we have attempted to communicate in this book is a global perspective—global not just in the sense of "worldwide," but also in the sense of "comprehensive." This dual meaning of the word *global* underlies a fundamental paradox of our modern world. As the world shrinks, the world with which we must deal expands. Our increasingly powerful communication tools and improved means of transportation are shrinking distances between people and cultures. This increased proximity expands the volume of information and the diversity and complexity of our environment. We must learn to cope not only with increased change but with an ever-increasing rate of change.

So, pardoxically, as our machines assume awesome abilities, the uniquely human ability to comprehend the whole becomes paramount. Our advantage as a species is our ability to adapt to a changing environment, to evolve beyond our physical limitations. These things we have not yet been able to teach our machines.

As the uniquely human assumes heightened importance, so does the interface between people. This, in its essence, is negotiation. In the past, the few individuals who ventured across

169

international borders had to learn to negotiate through cultural diversity and unfamiliar complexity. As borders vanish, the global perspective of these few is becoming a coping skill required of us all. Today, each of us must become a global negotiator.

With that, we would send you out into the world.

Appendix:
Illegal and Unethical Practices
in International Business

A greased mouth cannot say no.

—*Italian Proverb*

Few men have virtue to withstand the highest bidder.

—*George Washington*

As the economy of the United States continues to globalize, American business executives are increasingly venturing into foreign markets. These business executives are typically sent overseas with strong instructions "to get the business" with little or no guidance on how they should deal with the different ethical and legal requirements of foreign countries. Often, the individual business executive is left to his own devices in walking the ethical tightrope. He must balance "doing the right thing" (under U.S. standards) against getting the job done. Because this person's career and his family's well-being depend upon his job performance, he must often choose between what is ethical and what is profitable. Examining the ethical dilemmas faced by U.S. business executives when doing business internationally requires two levels of analysis.

171

The first level of analysis concerns whether the proposed action is legal. The solution here is pretty straightforward. It's like the classic statement of legal ethics: If it's a question of your client going to jail or you going to jail, make sure it's the client. Similarly, if it's a question of losing the business or going to jail, lose the business.

If business executives do not understand what U.S. law requires, they may be exposing themselves to criminal and civil penalties under the Foreign Corrupt Practices Act (FCPA). Penalties for individuals under the FCPA can be as much as $100,000 and five years in jail for each violation. An employer may also find itself subject to criminal and civil penalties. U.S. companies can receive fines of as much as $2 million for each violation and may be stripped of their export privileges.

The FCPA was enacted by Congress in 1977 during the presidency of Jimmy Carter to regulate questionable or illegal business practices of U.S. companies. The FCPA has been applauded by some for upholding American ethical standards and condemned by others as representing ethnocentric American imperialism that critically handicaps the activities of U.S. businesses dealing in foreign markets. The critics of the FCPA have a point. There is no universal standard of ethical conduct. What is ethical or moral varies markedly between cultures. The gratuity that Americans expect to pay for service in a hotel or restaurant will be considered a bribe in some other cultures. The hiring of an ex-bureaucrat for a do-nothing position is perfectly appropriate in some countries but an unethical practice in the United States. Is an African's request for a shortwave radio before doing business a bribe if social custom demands that he hold a large banquet in your honor that he cannot afford? Using America's definition of ethical conduct in another culture often results in not only inappropriate behavior but unnecessarily lost profits.

The FCPA's antibribery provisions will be violated if each of the following circumstances exist: (1) a U.S. company, its shareholders, directors, agents, officers, or employees; (2) act in furtherance of an offer, payment, or promise to pay money or anything of value; (3) to a foreign official, political party, political party official, or candidate for political office (collectively "foreign official"); (4) for the purpose of influencing any act or decision of such person in his or her official capacity (including a decision to fail to perform his or her official functions) or inducing the foreign official to do or omit to do any act in violation of his or her legal duty as a foreign official; and (5) in order to assist the U.S. company in obtaining or retaining business for or with, or directing business, to any person or to assist the company in obtaining special preferential treatment with respect to existing contracts or other business operations in the foreign country. Liability under the antibribery provisions of the FCPA may arise even if the individual did not have actual knowledge of a violation. If the individual is aware of circumstances that cause him or her to suspect that there is a high probability of the existence of a violation, the individual and the company could be held liable under the FCPA.

An American company that adopts an ostrich approach to the legal problems arising in the conduct of international business cannot escape liability. Suppose a U.S. company desperately wants a big contract in a foreign country. It hires a "consultant" who has a reputation for questionable business conduct and pays him or her a large consulting fee up front. The U.S. company writes the consultant and says: "This contract is very important to our company. While you should not pay any bribes, you should get the job done." A week later the consultant cables the U.S. company for "more money." Without asking questions, the U.S. firm cables the requested funds. Under the newly amended FCPA, prohibited conduct now includes "conscious disregard" or "willful blindness" in situations where there is a conscious intent to avoid learning the truth. In plain English, a head-in-the-sand approach to the legal problems that arise in doing business abroad will not avoid FCPA liability.

A transaction does not not violate the FCPA if: (1) the payment, gift, offer, or promise of anything of value that was made was lawful under the written laws and regulations of the country. It is not sufficient that the payment is "customary" if the payment violates a written law of the country; or (2) the payment, gift, offer, or promise of anything of value that was made was a reasonable and bona fide expenditure, such as travel and lodging expenses, incurred by or on behalf of a foreign official, and was directly related to the promotion, demonstration, or explanation of products or services, or the execution or performance of a contract with a foreign government or agency thereof.

In some foreign countries it is possible to make a facilitating or expediting payment to a foreign official to secure the performance of a routine governmental action by a foreign official. The scope of *routine governmental actions* is limited to actions that are ordinarily and commonly performed by a foreign official in (1) obtaining permits, licenses, or other official documents to qualify a person to do business in a foreign country; (2) processing governmental papers, such as visas and work orders; (3) providing police protection, mail pickup and delivery, or scheduling inspections associated with contract performance or inspections related to transit of goods across country; (4) providing phone service, power and water supply, loading and unloading cargo, or protecting perishable products or commodities from deterioration; or (5) actions of a similar nature. The definition of *routine governmental action* does not include any decision by a foreign official regarding whether, or on what terms, to award new business to or to continue doing business with the company, or any action taken by a foreign official involved in the decision-making process to encourage a decision to award new business to or to continue doing business with the company.

The FCPA also requires that a U.S. company maintain books and records that would evidence any violation of the antibribery provisions. Under the accounting standards requirements of the FCPA, a company must maintain books and records that, in reasonable detail, accurately and fairly reflect the transactions of the company and the disposition of its assets. To assure the accuracy of all financial records, the FCPA requires companies to devise and maintain an adequate system of internal accounting controls.

On its face, the FCPA does not specifically subject subsidiaries of a U.S. company that are incorporated under the law of a foreign country and that have their principal place of business outside the United States to the antibribery restrictions. It is arguable that the antibribery provisions do not apply to such subsidiaries. Nevertheless, as a policy matter, prudent senior management of a U.S. company will require foreign subsidiaries to comply with the antibribery provisions of the FCPA even if not expressly required to do so. The FCPA's provisions were recently revised to eliminate a company's responsibility for acts of a foreign subsidiary that may violate the accounting standard requirements if it holds 50 percent or less of the voting control, provided that a "good faith effort" is made to cause the subsidiary to comply with the statutory requirement.

The second level of analysis involves determining whether a particular action is ethically acceptable. What is legal is not necessarily ethical. Legal standards establish consensus minimal standards of behavior. Those individuals who violate this minimum standard are subject to criminal punishment. But conduct that is not criminal needs to be examined to determine whether it passes ethical muster. An ethical business executive often does more than is legally required. Similarly, determining whether an action is ethical is done separately from determining whether an action is good business.

The views of academics who have studied the ethical problems in international business fall along a spectrum with ethical relativists on one end and ethical absolutists on the other. The Marquis de Sade posed the following question for those who challenge moral relativism:

> Should I retain any feeling of guilt for having committed a crime in France which is nothing but a virtue in China? Should I make myself miserable about practicing actions in France which would have me burned in Siam?

Ethical relativists believe that there are no universal ethical principles and that all value judgments are relative to any given culture. To a relativist, what is thought right is right. Ethical absolutists believe that there is a single universal moral standard. To an absolutist what is right and what is thought to be right are not necessarily the same. Taken to the extreme, ethical relativism would grant each individual a claim to be judged by no standard but his or her own. The problem with ethical absolutism is the practical problem of determining which ethical principles apply universally.

Some American business executives have adopted a variation of the "when in Rome, do as the Romans do" philosophy in resolving ethical problems. Even if we set aside for the moment the question of whether actions taken pursuant to this policy violate U.S. law, the "when in Rome" approach can produce a result that is morally repugnant. The "when in Rome" approach would have the U.S. business executives establishing apartheid-based policies in South Africa, institutionalizing gender-based discrimination in some Arab countries, and paying bribes to government officials in many Third World countries. In making a determination about whether a particular action is ethical, one must consider as part of the harm the loss of organizational integrity caused by violating the rule.

So where does this leave the U.S. company? How can the ethical issues that inevitably arise in international business be resolved? First, senior management must take responsibility for creating a corporate culture that fosters organizational integrity and for setting out in writing the company's principles and objectives. Some ethical standards, such as a company prohibition against discrimination, should be inviolate. Other ethical standards may need exceptions. For example, some types of "grease" payments that fall within the requirements of the FCPA may be permissible. In other words, some ethical standards are categorical and exceptions must not be permitted. Other ethical standards are prima facie and may be violated if the harm caused by violating the standard is outweighed by the benefit produced by breaking the rule. Applying a prima facie ethical standard to a specific situation requires an evaluation of the particular facts and circumstances of each case. Employees must learn to exercise **judgment** in determining whether an action is consistent with the company's ethical standards without being **judgmental** about the values of another culture. This is not an easy task but a necessary one.

Although no bright-line tests exist for determining whether overseas corporate conduct is legal or ethical, it is clear that going to the effort of establishing an international business conduct compliance program has intrinsic value. Both the U.S. government and the courts look much more favorably on companies that have made a good faith effort to ensure compliance with the law. Those companies that adopt an ostrich approach to international ethical problems or intentionally violate the law will be subject to far more severe penalties.

Suggested Readings and Bibliography

Acuff, F. L., and Villere, M. "Games Negotiators Play." *Business Horizons* 1a (1976): 70.

Adler, N. J. "Cross-cultural Management Research: The Ostrich and the Trend." *Academy of Management Review* 8 (April 1983): 226–32.

Allard, S. *Russia and the Austrian State Treaty.* Pennsylvania State University Press, 1970.

Aronson, S. *Conflict and Bargaining in the Middle East.* Johns Hopkins University Press, 1978.

Asante, S. K. B. "Restructuring Transnational Mineral Agreements." *American Journal of International Law* 73 (1979): 335–71.

Bacharach, S., and Lawler, E. *Bargaining: Power, Tactics and Outcomes.* Jossey-Bass, 1981.

Balobkins, N. *West German Reparations to Israel.* 1974.

Bartos, O. J. *Process and Outcome of Negotiations.* Columbia University Press, 1974.

Bazerman, M. H. "Negotiator Judgment," *American Behavioral Scientists* 27 (1983): 211–28.

Bazerman, M. H., and Lewicki, R. J. *Negotiating in Organizations.* Sage, 1983.

Beckmen, N. *Negotiations, Principles and Techniques.* Lexington Books, 1977.

Belliare, E., Mullen, T., and Punnett, B. J. "Understanding the Cultural Environment: USA/USSR Trade Negotiations." *California Management Review*, Winter 1985, pp. 100–112.

Bellow, G., and Moulton, B., *Negotiation*, Foundation Press, 1981.

Bendahmane, D., and McDonald, J. *Perspectives on Negotiation.* Department of State Publication, 1986.

Benedict, R. *The Chrysanthemum and the Sword.* Mentor, 1946.

Bennett, D. C., and Sharpe, K. E. "Agenda Setting and Bargaining Power: The Mexican State Versus Transnational Automobile Corporations." *World Politics* 32 (1979): 57–89.

Binnendijk, H. *National Negotiating Styles.* Foreign Service Institute, U.S. Department of State, 1987.

Birnbaum, P. "Humoring the Japanese." *Across the Board* 23 (1986): 10.

Blaker, M. "Probe, Push and Panic: The Japanese Tactical Style in International Negotiations." *Foreign Policy of Modern Japan.* University of California Press, 1977.

———. *Japanese International Negotiating Style.* Columbia University Press, 1977.

Bramson, R. M. *Coping with Difficult People.* Ballantine, 1981.

Brazil, W. B. *Effective Approaches to Settlement: A Handbook for Lawyers and Judges.* Prentice-Hall, 1988.

Calero, H. H. *Negotiate the Deal You Want.* Dodd Mead, 1983.

———. *Winning the Negotiation.* Hawthorn Books, 1979.

Callières, F. De. *On the Manner of Negotiating with Princes.* Paris: Michel Brunet, 1716; translated by A. F. Whyte, Houghton Mifflin, 1919; Reprint Notre Dame Press, 1963.

Campbell, N. *China Strategies: The Inside Story.* University of Hong Kong, 1986.

Campbell, N., Graham, J. L., Jolibert, A., and Meissner, H. G. "Marketing Negotiations in France, Germany, the United Kingdom, and the United States." *Journal of Marketing* 52 (1988): 49.

Carter, J. C. *Negotiation, the Alternative to Hostility.* Mercer University Press, 1984.

———. "Principles of Negotiation." *Stanford Journal of International Law* 23 (1987): 1–12.

Cateora, P. R. *International Marketing.* Irwin, 1987.

Charell, R. *How to Get the Upper Hand.* Avon, 1979.

Christopher, R. *Second to None: American Companies in Japan.* Crown, 1986.

Chu, Chin-ning. *The Chinese Mind Game*. AMC Publishing, 1988.

Clopton, S. W. "Seller and Buying Firm Factors Affecting Industrial Buyers' Negotiation Behavior and Outcomes." *Journal of Marketing Research* 21 (1984): 39–53.

Coddington, A. *Theories of the Bargaining Process*. Aldine Publishing Co., 1968.

Coffin, R. A. *The Negotiator: A Manual for Winners*. Harper & Row, 1976.

Cohen, H. *You Can Negotiate Anything*. Lyle Stuart, 1980.

Cohen, J. "Negotiating Complex Contracts with China." *Business Transactions with China, Japan and South Korea*. Edited by P. Saney and H. Smit. Matthew Bender, 1983.

Cohn, Roy. *How to Stand Up for Your Rights and Win*. Simon & Schuster, 1981.

Condlin, R. J. "Cases on Both Sides: Patterns of Argument in Legal Dispute-Negotiations." *Maryland Law Review* 44 (1985): 65–136.

Condon, J. C. *Interact: Guidelines for Mexicans and North Americans*. Intercultural Press, 1980.

Copeland, L., and Griggs, L. *Going International: How to Make Friends and Deal Effectively in the Marketplace*. Random House, 1985.

Coughlin, E. K., "Making the Deal." *Chronicles of Higher Education* 23 (1988): 4.

Craver, C. B. *Effective Legal Negotiation and Settlement*. Michie, 1986.

Crosby, P. *The Art of Getting Your Own Sweet Way*. McGraw-Hill, 1981.

Cross, J. *The Economics of Bargaining*. Basic Books, 1969.

Dawson, R. *You Can Get Anything You Want, But You Have to Do More Than Ask*. Simon & Schuster, 1987.

De Mente, B. *The Japanese Way of Doing Business*. Prentice-Hall, 1981.

———. *Korean Etiquette & Ethics and Business*. National Textbook, 1988.

Dennet, R. and Johnson, J. *Negotiation with the Russians*. World Peace Foundation, 1951.

Deutsch, M. *The Resolution of Conflict*. Yale University Press, 1973.

Dorcey, A. H. J. *Bargaining in the Governance of Pacific Coastal Resources: Research and Reform*. University of British Columbia, 1986.

Druckman, D. *Human Factors in International Negotiation*. Foreign Service Institute, 1979.

———. *Negotiations: Social Psychological Perspectives*. Sage Publications, 1977.

Dwyer, F. R., and Walker, O. C., Jr. "Bargaining in an Asymmetrical Power Structure." *Journal of Marketing* 45 (1981): 104–15.

The Economist Business Traveller's Guides: Japan. Prentice-Hall, 1987.

The Economist Business Traveller's Guides: Southeast Asia. Prentice-Hall, 1988.

Edwards, H. T., and White, H. J. *The Lawyer as a Negotiator.* West Publishing Co., 1977.

Eigen, M., and Winkler, R., *Laws of the Game.* Harper & Row, 1981, 1983.

Fallows, J., *More Like Us: Making America Great Again.* Houghton Mifflin, 1989.

Fayerweather, J., and Kapoor, A. *Strategy and Negotiation for the International Corporation.* Ballinger, 1976.

Fisher, G. *The Cross-Cultural Dimension in International Negotiations.* Foreign Service Institute, 1979.

———. *International Negotiation: A Cross-Cultural Perspective.* Intercultural Press, 1980.

Fisher, R., "Fractionating Conflict." *International Conflict and Behavioral Science: The Craigville Papers.* Edited by R. Fisher. Basic Books, 1964, pp. 91–109.

Fisher, R., *International Conflict for Beginners.* Harper & Row, 1969.

———. "What About Negotiation as a Specialty?" *American Bar Association Journal* 69 (1983): 1221–24.

Fisher, R., and Brown, S. *Getting Together: Building a Relationship That Gets to Yes.* Houghton Mifflin, 1988.

Fisher, R., and Ury, W. *Getting to Yes: Negotiating Agreement Without Giving In.* Houghton Mifflin, 1981.

Fouraker, L. E., and Siegel, S. *Bargaining Behavior.* McGraw-Hill, 1963.

Frascogna, X. M. *Negotiation Strategy for Lawyers.* Prentice-Hall, 1984.

Goldberg, S. B., Green, E. D., and Sander, F. E. A. *Dispute Resolution.* Little, Brown, 1985.

Gould, J. S. *The Negotiator's Problem Solver.* Wiley, 1986.

Graham, J. L. "Business Negotiations in Japan, Brazil, and the United States." *Journal of International Business Studies* 14 (1983): 47–62.

———. "The Influence of Culture on the Process of Business Negotiations: An Exploratory Study." *Journal of International Studies,* Spring 1985, p. 59.

———. "The Problem-Solving Approach to Interorganizational Negotiations: A Laboratory Test." *Journal of Business Research* 14 (1986): 271–86.

Graham, J. L., and Herberger, R. A. "Negotiators Abroad—Don't Shoot from the Hip." *Harvard Business Review* 61 (1983): 160–68.

Graham, J. L., and Sano, Y. *Smart Bargaining: Doing Business with the Japanese.* Ballinger, 1984.

Griffin, T. J. *Korea: The Tiger Economy.* Euromoney, 1988.

Grubb, P. *The Multinational Enterprise in Transition.* Darwin Press, 1983.

Guetzkow, H., Alger, C. F, Brody, R. A., Noel, R. C., and Snyder, R. C. *Simulation in International Relations.* Prentice-Hall, 1963.

Gulliver, P. H. *Beyond Culture.* Anchor, 1976.

———. *Disputes and Negotiations: A Cross Cultural Perspective.* Academic Press, 1979.

———. *The Hidden Dimension.* Doubleday, 1966.

Hahn. "Negotiating with the Japanese." *California Lawyer*, March 1982, p. 36.

Hall, E. *Silent Language.* Doubleday, 1959.

Hall, H. T. *Hidden Differences: Doing Business With the Japanese.* Anchor Press, 1987.

Hanan, M. *Sales Negotiation Strategies.* AMACOM, 1977.

Harbaugh, J. D. *Negotiation: Winning Tactics and Techniques.* Practicing Law Institute, 1988.

Harnett, D. L., and Cummings, L. L. *Bargaining Behavior: An International Study.* Notre Dame Publications, 1980.

Harris, V. *A Book of Five Rings.* Translated by Miyamoto Musashi. Overlook Press, 1974.

Haydock, R. S. *Negotiation Practice.* Wiley, 1984.

Heller, J. W. "Unilateral Action in a Concession Bargaining Context." *Labor Law Journal* 35 (1984): 747–65.

Herman, P. *Better Settlements Through Leverage.* Aqueduct, 1985.

Hoellering, M. F. "International Transactions." *New York Law Journal* 199 (1988): 79.

Hofstede, G. *Culture's Consequences.* Sage, 1984.

Holmes, G. "Commercial Negotiation—Ancient Practice, Modern Philosophy." *Journal of Purchasing and Materials Management* 18 (1982): 2.

Huntington, I. K. *Doing Business in the Arab Middle East.* Peat, Marwick, Mitchell & Co., 1987.

Huyler, J. W. *Crisis Communications and Communicating About Negotiations*. EdCom, 1981.

Ilich, J. *The Art and Skill of Successful Negotiation*. Prentice-Hall, 1973.

———. *Power Negotiating*. Addison-Wesley, 1980.

Inkle, F. C. *How Nations Negotiate*. Harper & Row, 1964.

Irwin, R. D. *Negotiation: Readings, Exercises and Cases*. West Publishing, 1985.

Jacker, N. S. *Effective Negotiation Techniques for Lawyers*. National Institute for Trial Advocacy, 1983.

Jacobsen, G., and Hillkirk, J. *Xerox: American Samurai*. Macmillan, 1986.

Jacoby, N. H., Nehemkis, P. and Eells, R. *Bribery and Extortion in World Business*. Macmillan, 1977.

Jandt, F. W. *Win-Win Negotiating: Turning Conflict Into Agreement*. Wiley, 1985.

Jonsson, C. *Soviet Bargaining Behavior: The Nuclear Test Ban Case*. Columbia University Press, 1979.

Joy, C. T. *Doing Business Abroad*. Simon & Schuster, 1985.

———. *Everything is Negotiable: How to Get a Better Deal*. Prentice-Hall, 1983.

———. *How Communists Negotiate*. Macmillan, 1955.

Kampelman, M. Negotiating With the Soviets. *New York School of International and Comparative Law* 7 (1986): 39–43.

Kanungo, R. N. *Biculturism and Management*. Butterworth, 1980.

Kapoor, A. *Planning for International Business Negotiation*. Ballinger, 1974.

Karass, G. *Negotiate to Close: How to Make More Successful Deals*. Simon & Schuster, 1985.

Karrass, C. L. *Give & Take: The Complete Guide to Negotiating Strategies and Tactics*. Crowell Co., 1974.

———. *The Negotiating Game*. Crowell Co., 1970.

Kellar, R. E. *Sales Negotiating Handbook*. Prentice-Hall, 1988.

Kelman, H. C. *International Behavior: A Social Psychological Analysis*. Holt, Rinehart and Winston, 1965.

Kennedy, G. *Pocket Negotiator*. Blackwell, 1987.

Kennedy, G., Benson, J. and McMillan, J. *Managing Negotiations*. Spectrum, 1982.

Kent, G. *The Effect of Threats*. Ohio State University Press, 1967.

Kieffer, G. D. *The Strategy of Meetings*. Simon & Schuster, 1988.

Kissinger, H. A. *The Necessity of Choice*. Harper & Row, 1961.

———. "The Vietnam Negotiations." *Foreign Affairs* 47 (1969): 211–34.

———. *Years of Upheaval*. Little, Brown, 1982.

Kniveton, B. *Training for Negotiation: A Guide for Management and Employee Negotiators*. Business Books, 1978.

Kouzes, J. M., and Posner, B. Z. "The Leadership Challenge: How to Get Extraordinary Things Done in Originations." Jossey-Bass, 1987.

Korda, M. *Power: How to Get It, How to Use It*. Random House, 1975.

Kuhn, R. L. *Dealmaker: All the Negotiating Skills and Secrets You Need*. Wiley, 1988.

Lall, A. *Modern International Negotiation*. Columbia University Press, 1966.

Lax, D. A., and Sebenious, J. K. *The Manager as Negotiator*. Free Press, 1986.

Lee, J. A. "Cultural Analysis in Overseas Operations." *Harvard Business Review*, March/April 1966, pp. 106–11.

Lewicki, R. J., and Litterer, J. A. *Negotiation*. Irwin, 1985.

Lewis, D. V. *Power Negotiating Tactics and Techniques*. Prentice-Hall, 1981.

Levin, E. *Levin's Laws: Tactics for Winning Without Intimidation*. M. Evans Press, 1980.

———. *Negotiating Tactics: Bargain Your Way to Winning*. Fawcett, 1982.

Leritz, L. *No-Fault Negotiating: A Simple and Innovative Approach for Solving Problems, Reaching Agreements and Resolving Conflicts*. Pacific Press, 1987.

Liebert, R. M., Smith, W. P., Hill, J. H., and Kieffer, M. "The Effects of Information and Magnitude of Initial Offer on Interpersonal Negotiation." *Journal of Experimental Social Psychology* 4 (1968): 431–41.

Linton, R. *The Cultural Background of Personality*. Appleton-Century-Crofts, 1945.

Locke, W. W. "The Fatal Flaw: Hidden Cultural Differences." *Business Marketing*, April 1986, pp. 65–76.

Lockhart, C. *Bargaining in International Conflicts*. Columbia University Press, 1979.

Maccoby, M. *The Gamesman*. Simon & Schuster, 1978.

McCormak, M. *What They Don't Teach You at Harvard Business School.* Bantam, 1984.

McCreary, D. D. *Japanese–U.S. Business Negotiations: A Cross-Cultural Study.* Praeger, 1986.

McDonald, J. W., and Bendahmane, D. B., eds. *How to Be a Delegate.* United States Foreign Service Institute, 1984.

———. *International Negotiation: Art and Science.* United States Foreign Service Institute, 1984.

———. *Perspectives on Negotiation.* United States Foreign Service Institute, 1986.

Machiavelli, N. *The Prince and the Discourses.* Random House, 1950.

Macleod, R. *China, Inc.: How to do Business with the Chinese.* Bantam Books, 1988.

Maddux, R. B. *Successful Negotiation: Effective "Win-Win" Strategies and Tactics.* Crisp, 1988.

Malone, M. *Psychotypes.* Pocket Books, 1977.

March, R. M. *The Japanese Negotiator: Subtlety and Strategy Beyond Western Logic.* Kodansha International, 1988.

Masaki, I. *Never Take Yes For an Answer.* Simul Press, 1975.

Menkel-Meadow. "Toward Another View of Legal Negotiation: The Structure of Problem Solving." *U.C.L.A. L. Rev.* 31 (1984): 754.

Moran, R. T. *Getting Your Yen's Worth: How to Negotiate with Japan, Inc.* Gulf Publishing Co., 1985.

Morgenthau, H. J. "The Art of Diplomatic Negotiation." *The State of the Social Sciences.* Edited by L. White. University of Chicago Press, 1956.

———. *Politics Among Nations: The Struggle for Power and Peace.* Knopf, 1960.

Morley, I., and Stephenson, G. *The Social Psychology of Bargaining.* George Allen and Unwin Publishers Ltd., 1977.

Nader, L., and Todd, H. F., eds. *The Disputing Process: Law in Ten Societies.* Columbia University Press, 1978.

Neal, R. G. *Bargaining Tactics: A Reference Manual for Public Sector Labor Negotiations.* Richard Neal Associates, 1980.

Neale, M. A. *Bargaining and Dispute Resolution Curricula.* Eno River Press, 1985.

Nicolson, Sir H. *Diplomacy.* Butterworth, 1939.

Nierenberg, G. I. *The Art of Negotiating: Psychological Strategies for Gaining Advantageous Bargains.* Cornerstone Library, 1968.

————. *The Complete Negotiator*. Hawthorn, 1986.

————. *Creative Business Negotiating: Skills and Successful Strategies*. Hawthorn Books, 1971.

————. *Fundamentals of Negotiations*. Hawthorn Books, 1973.

Nierenberg, G. I., and Calero, H. H. *How to Read a Person Like a Book*. Cornerstone Library Publications, 1971.

Nothdurft, K. H. *The Complete Guide to Successful Business Negotiation*. Leviathan House, 1974.

Ocran, T. M. "The Process and Outcome of Negotiations With Multinational Corporations." *Akron Law Review* 18 (1985): 405–34.

Osgood, C. *An Alternative to War or Surrender*. University of Illinois Press, 1962.

Pascale, R. T., and Athos, A. G. *The Art of Japanese Management*. Simon & Schuster, 1981.

Patrick, K. *International Technological Negotiations and Outer Space*. Center for Foreign Policy Studies, Dalhousie University, 1984.

Perk, C. *Cases and Materials on Negotiation*. Belknap/Harvard, 1982.

Pillar, P. R. *Negotiating Peace: War Termination as a Bargaining Process*. Princeton University Press, 1983.

Pooler, V. H. *Developing the Negotiating Skills of the Buyer*. American Management Association, 1964.

Posluns, R. J. *Negotiate Your Way to Financial Success*. Putnam, 1987.

Pruitt, D. G. "Achieving Integrative Agreements." *Negotiation in Organization*. Edited by M. H. Bazerman and R. J. Lewecki. Sage, 1983.

————. *The Art and Science of Negotiation*. Belknap/Harvard, 1982.

————. *Negotiation Behavior*. Academic Press, 1981.

————. "Strategic Choice in Negotiation." *American Behavioral Scientist* 27 (2[1983]): 167–94.

Pruitt, D. G., and Lewis, S. A. "Development of Integrative Solution in Bilateral Negotiation." *Journal of Personality and Social Psychology* 31 (4[1975]): 621–33.

Pye, L. *Chinese Commercial Negotiation, A Cross-Cultural Perspective*. Oelgeschlager, Gunn & Hain, 1982.

Ramundo, B. A. *Effective Negotiation: A Primer*. National Law Center, George Washington University, 1984.

Rand, J. B. *Negotiation: An Integrative Perspective*. Idaho Law Foundation, 1987.

Rapoport, A. *Fights, Games and Debates.* University of Michigan Press, 1960.

Rapoport, A., and Chammah, A. M. *Prisoner's Dilemma.* University of Michigan Press, 1956.

Renniger, J. P. *The Eleventh Special Session and the Future of Global Negotiations.* U.N. Institute for Training and Research, 1981.

Riaffa, H. *The Art and Science of Negotiation.* Belknap/Harvard, 1982.

Ricks, D. A. *Big Business Blunders.* Dow-Jones-Irwin, 1983.

Rieke, R. D., and Sillars, M. O. *Argumentation and the Decision Making Process.* Wiley, 1975.

Ringer, R. J. *Winning Through Intimidation.* Fawcett Publications, 1974.

Roett, R. *Dialogue and Armed Conflict: Negotiating the Civil War in El Salvador.* Johns Hopkins University, 1988.

Ross, L. H. *Settled Out of Court: The Social Process of Insurance Claims Adjustment.* 2d rev. ed. Aldine Publishing Co., 1980.

Ross, R. S. *Persuasion: Communication and Interpersonal Relations.* Prentice-Hall, 1974.

Rossman, M. L. *The International Businesswoman.* Praeger, 1986.

Roth, R. *International Marketing Communications.* Irwin Press, 1983.

Rothstein, R. L. *Global Bargaining: UNCTAD and the Quest for a New International Economic Order.* Princeton University Press, 1979.

Rowland, D. *Japanese Business Etiquette, A Practical Guide to Success with the Japanese.* Warner, 1985.

Rubin, J. Z. "Psychological Traps." *Psychology Today* 15 (1981): 52.

Rubin, J. Z., and Brown, B. *The Social Psychology of Bargaining and Negotiation.* Academic Press, 1975.

Reusch, J. *Knowledge in Action.* Jason Aronson, 1975.

Rusk, D., "Parliamentary Diplomacy—Debate Versus Negotiation." *World Affairs Interpreter* (1955).

Samuelson, W. "First Offer Bargains." *Management Science* 26 (1980): 155–64.

Sawyer, J., and Guetzkow, H. "Bargaining and Negotiations in International Relations." *International Behavior: A Social-Psychological Analysis.* Edited by H. C. Kelman. Holt, Rinehart and Winston, 1965, pp. 466–520.

Satow, E. M. *A Guide to Diplomatic Practice.* McKay, 1957.

———. *Negotiating the Law of the Sea.* Harvard University Press, 1984.

Schatzki, M. *Negotiation: The Art of Getting What You Want.* New American Library, 1981.

Schelling, T. C. *The Strategy of Conflict.* Harvard University Press, 1980.

Schmidt, K. D. *Doing Business in Mexico.* SRI International, Menlo Park, Calif., 1980.

Schoenfield, M. K. and Schoenfield, R. M. *Legal Negotiations: Getting Maximum Result.* Shepard's McGraw-Hill, 1988.

Schweitzer, S. *Winning Through Deception and Bluff.* Prentice-Hall, 1972.

Scott, W. P. *The Skills of Negotiating.* Gower, 1981.

Seltz, D. D. *Negotiate Your Way to Success.* Farnsworth Publishing Co., 1980.

Seurat, S. *Technology Transfer.* Gulf Publishing, 1979.

Shea, G. F. *Creative Negotiating.* CBI Pub. Co., 1983.

Sherkar, O. and Ronen, S. "The Cultural Context of Negotiations: The Implications of Chinese Interpersonal Norms." *Journal of Applied Behavioral Science* 23 (1987): 263.

Siegel, S. and Fouraker, L. *Bargaining and Group Decision-Making.* McGraw-Hill, 1960.

Sloss, L., and Davis, S. M. *A Game for High Stakes: Lessons Learned from Negotiating with the Soviet Union.* Ballinger, 1986.

Smith, D., and Wells, L., *Negotiating Third World Mineral Agreements.* Ballinger, 1975.

Snowdon, S. *The Global Edge: How Your Company Can Win in the International Marketplace.* Simon & Schuster, 1986.

Solomon, R. H. *Chinese Political Negotiating Behavior.* Rand Corporation, 1985.

Sparks, D. B. *The Dynamics of Effective Negotiation.* Gulf Publishing, 1982.

Sperber, P. *Attorney's Practice Guide to Negotiations.* Callaghan, 1985.

———. *Fail-Safe Business Negotiating Strategies and Tactics for Success.* Prentice-Hall, 1983.

———. *The Science of Business Negotiation.* Pilot Books, 1979.

Stanford, B., ed., *Peacemaking: A Guide to Conflict Resolution.* Bantam, 1976.

Steele, W. W., Jr. "Deceptive Negotiating and High-Toned Morality." *Vanderbilt Law Review* 39 (1986): 1387–1404.

Stone, J. *Strategic Persuasion.* Columbia University Press, 1967.

Strauss, A. L. *Negotiations: Varieties, Contexts, Processes, and Social Order.* Jossey-Bass, 1978.

Sun Tzu. *The Art of War*. American House, 1988.

Tarrant, J. J. *How to Negotiate a Raise*. Van Nostrand Reinhold, 1976.

Tedeschi, J. T., Schlenker, B. R., and Bonoma, T. V. *Conflict, Power and Games*. Aldine, 1973.

Terchek, R. J. *The Making of the Test Ban Treaty*. The Hague: Martinus Nijhoff, 1970.

Thompson, L. L., Mannix, E. A., and Bazerman, M. H. "Group Negotiation: Effect of Decision Rule, Agenda and Aspiration." *Journal of Personality and Social Psychology* 54 (1988): 86.

Tollison, R. D., and Willett, T. A. "An Economic Theory of Mutually Advantageous Issue Linkages in International Negotiations." *International Organization* 33 (1979): 425–449.

———. "Institutional Mechanisms for Dealing with International Externalities: A Public Choice Perspective." *Law of the Sea: U.S. Interests and Alternatives*. Edited by R. C. Amacher and R. J. Sweeney. American Enterprise Institute for Public Policy Research, 1976, pp. 77–101.

Tomlinson, J. R. "Conducting Negotiations." *Litigation* 13 (1[1987]): 4.

Torrington, D., *Face to Face*. Gower Press, 1972.

Tung, R. L. "How to Negotiate with the Japanese." *California Management Review* 26 (4[1984]): 62–77.

———. *The New Expatriates: Managing Human Resources Abroad*. Ballinger, 1988.

———. "U.S.-China Trade Negotiations: Practices, Procedures, and Outcomes." *Journal of International Business Studies* 13 (1982): 25–28.

Turner, J. C. *How Communists Negotiate*. Macmillan, 1955.

———. *How Communists Negotiate*. Fideli's Publishers, 1970.

———. *Negotiating While Fighting: The Diary of Admiral Turner at the Korean Armistice Conference*. Hoover Institute Press, 1978.

Van Zandt, "How to Negotiate in Japan." *Harvard Business Review* 6 (1970): 45.

Viscott, D. *Taking Care of Business*. Morrow, 1985.

Von Neumann, J., and Morgenstein, O. *The Theory of Games and Economic Behavior*. J. Wiley, 1972.

Wall, J. A., Jr. *Negotiation: Theory and Practice*. Scott, Foresman, 1985.

Wallace, W. "Issue Linkages Among Atlantic Governments." *International Affairs* 52 (1976): 163–79.

Walton, R. E. *Behavioral Theory of Labor Negotiations.* McGraw-Hill, 1965.

———. *Interpersonal Peacemaking: Confrontation and Third Party Consultation.* Addison-Wesley, 1969.

Walton, R. E., and McKersie, R. B. "Bargaining Dilemmas in Mixed-Motive Decision Making." *Behavioral Science* 11 (1966): 370–84.

Warschaw, T. A. *Winning by Negotiation.* Berkley Books, 1981.

Waterman, R., Jr. *The Renewal Factor, How the Best Get the Competitive Edge.* Bantam, 1987.

Watts, "Briefing the American Negotiator in Japan." *International Lawyer* 16 (1983): 597.

Wenke, R. *The Art of Negotiation for Lawyers.* Richter, 1985.

Wertsch, J. V., ed. *Culture, Communication and Cognition.* Cambridge University Press, 1985.

Whelen, J. *Soviet Diplomacy and Negotiating Behavior.* Westview Press, 1987.

Whitney, C. *Win-Win Negotiating for Couples.* Para Research, 1986.

Williams, G. R. *Handbook on Effectiveness of Legal Negotiation.* Drake University Law School, 1977.

———. *Legal Negotiations and Settlement.* West, 1983.

Winkler, J. *Bargaining for Results.* Facts on File, 1984.

Yerachmiel, K., and Gruenberg, G. W. *International Payoffs.* Lexington Books, 1977.

Young, O. R. *Bargaining: Formal Theories of Negotiation.* University of Illinois Press, 1975.

———. *The Politics of Force; Bargaining During International Crises.* Princeton University Press, 1968.

Zartman, I. W. *The 50% Solution: How to Bargain Successfully with Hijackers, Strikers, Bosses, Oil Magnates, Arabs, Russians, and Other Worthy Opponents in This Modern World.* Anchor Press/Doubleday, 1976.

———. "Negotiations: Theory and Reality." *Journal of International Affairs* 29 (1975): 69–77.

———. "The Political Analysis of Negotiations." *World Politics* 26 (1974): 385–99.

————, ed. *The Negotiation Process: Theories and Applications.* Sage Publications, 1978.

Zartman, I. W., and Berman, M. *The Practical Negotiator.* Yale University Press, 1982.

Zimmerman, M. *How to Do Business With the Japanese.* Random House, 1985.

Index

193

Information
revealing, 122
trial balloon, 162
Informational communication, 93
Information gathering, as negotiation
strategy, 60
Interests vs. positions, 16–19
examples of, 16–19
Interpreters, 41–49
effective use of, 45–49
vs. translators, 42–43
unnecessary use, as negotiation tactic,
44–45
Interruption, of speaker, 123–124
Intuitive style of negotiation, disadvan-
tages of, 2, 5
Italian-style tax return, 80–81

Japan/Japanese
banana sale approach to bargaining,
79–80
communication problems and, 54
first proposals, nature of, 80
as high context culture, 54
initial meeting, 94
U.S. competition and, 24–25
John Wayne approach, 110–111

Karajan, Herbert von, 147
King, Martin Luther, Jr., 141
Kipling, Rudyard, 60
Kissinger, Henry, 110, 113
Koreans, negotiation with, 88–89

Language, English as official corporate
language, 40–41
Language barriers
in negotiation process, 39–49
using interpreters, 41–49
Lao Tzu, 149
Leaders (Nixon), 45
Legal issues
lawsuit as last resort, 90
legal standards, meaning of, 175
maintaining leverage as protection, 90–
91
non-violating acts of FCPA, 173–174
ostrich approach to, 173
securing routine governmental actions
in foreign country, 174

violation of antibribery laws, 172–173
Leverage
vs. litigation, 90
maintaining leverage as protection, 90–
91
as negotiation strategy, 86–92
use of alternatives for, 86–92
Liman, Arthur, 108
Lincoln, Abraham, 117–118
Listening skills
context of information, 53–54
importance of, 50, 51, 52
improving, 51–52
Litigation vs. leverage, 90
Liz Claiborne, 164–165
Location of negotiation, influence of, 65

McDonald, John W., 155
Maximum credible position, as negotia-
tion strategy, 77–86
Mediation approach, conflict resolution,
158–159
More Like Us (Fallows), 43
Mulford, David, 97
Multilateral circular exchanges, 22
Murville, Maurice-Jacques Couve de, 88
Musashi, Miyamoto, 95
Mutual interest, creation of, 165–166
Mutually beneficial relationship, main-
taining, 163–168

National Negotiating Styles (Thayer and
Weiss), 79–80
Negotiating skills
competition vs. cooperation, 20, 24–27
personal contact, 56–57
preparation, 59–71
Negotiating with the Soviets (Smith), 53
Negotiation plan, 61–62
guidelines for flexible plan, 61
revision of, 62
Negotiation process
awareness of, 2
basic law of negotiation, 87
claiming value, 20–27
communication, 35–38
competition vs. cooperation, 20, 24–27
conflict resolution, 154–163
creating value, 20–27
first offer in, 83–84